THE KEYS TO UNLOCKING YOUR
GOD-GIVEN DREAM

J. ASHLEY JENSEN

Copyright ©2018 J. Ashley Jensen
All rights reserved.
ISBN-13: 978-0692853924 (Jensen Creative Media)
ISBN-10: 0692853928

This is dedicated to the dreamers. The ones with their head in the clouds looking for something greater than themselves. This is a labor of love for those who believe in the dream our great God has for them.

TABLE OF CONTENTS

INTRODUCTION		7
CHAPTER 1	The Gift of a Dream	17
CHAPTER 2	Dream Deficiency Syndrome	37
CHAPTER 3	The Process of a Dream	61
CHAPTER 4	Breaking the Dreamer	83
CHAPTER 5	Dream Roadblocks	97
CHAPTER 6	Stewarding the Dream	123
CHAPTER 7	The Realization of the Dream	151

INTRODUCTION

WE ALL HAVE A DREAM

It all happened so quickly. The worst week of my life.

I was flying home from a ministry trip, not knowing what I was about to discover. When I pulled into my driveway everything seemed normal, but as I walked into my house, I realized everything was gone. My family was gone, my furniture was gone, my bank account was empty, my church had closed down, my relationships were destroyed. At that moment, I was on the verge of suicide. I had brought devastation to many lives around me because of the choices I had made and I was completely disappointed in myself. My life as I knew it was over.

Total devastation. The dream I wanted to live was dead – or so I thought. I was reminded of this story…

1 Samuel 30:1-6 NIV
David and his men reached Ziklag on the third day. Now the Amalekites had raided the Negev and Ziklag. They had attacked Ziklag and burned it, and had taken captive the women and everyone else in it, both young and old. They killed none of them, but carried them off as they went on their way. When David and his men reached Ziklag, they found it destroyed by fire and their wives and sons and daughters taken captive. So David and his men wept aloud until they had no strength left to weep. David's two wives had been captured—Ahinoam of Jezreel and Abigail, the widow of Nabal of Carmel. David was greatly distressed because the men were talking of stoning him; each one was bitter in spirit because of his sons and daughters. But David found strength in the Lord his God.

As I stood in that empty house, my heart felt just as empty. I did the only thing I knew to do. I prayed and cried out to God for mercy. I did what David did. I wept, I screamed, I threw myself completely on the mercy of God. I prayed like I never prayed before. I sought the Lord with all my heart, and at that moment God responded. Oh, how He responded! Just me standing in that house all alone, the Holy Spirit came on me like I've never experienced before. He overwhelmed me with His presence, His power, and His peace. I knew it was going to be ok. As the tears flowed, the Holy Spirit comforted me, right there in my brokenness, God so graciously reminded me of the great dream He put on my life.

It was God who called me into this new life, not anyone else.

Like David, I found my strength.

Not at first, but over time as I continued to seek the Lord, God strengthened me, healed me, and eventually restored me. It wasn't an easy journey towards restoration, but it was the journey I had to take in order to fulfill the dream God had put in my heart so long ago. Slowly but surely, that dream started to come alive. I started to dream again. The seeds of God's great dream started to germinate, take root, and began to grow again.

Years later, I look back at that season and just shake my head in awe because of the goodness of God. God is a Redeemer and He is a Restorer of dreams. You may have experienced what seemed like the death of a dream, or maybe you have allowed your dream to sit on the shelf and get dusty. Maybe you feel like your dream is locked up and just out of reach. Regardless of your circumstances, I fully believe we've all been given a dream.

It's amazing to think that as little kids, when our second grade teacher asks, "What do you want to be when you grow up?" We don't have any basis for our answer. We have no experience, no talent that we know of, we don't really even know God intimately yet, so the answer is based off of our imagination, how we picture ourselves. Some kids raise their hands and want to be a firefighter, policeman, a teacher, a doctor, and of course one or two kids always say they want to be president. No one ever says they want to be a drug addict or divorced, and no little kid says they want to be bankrupt or in debt.

The stuff dreams are made of begins with pure, unadulterated, anointed imagination and vision. A big dream is always accompanied by a big vision, but the process – well, that's a different story.

That's what this book is about. The process of a dream.

God has used men and woman throughout the ages by giving them a dream and a vision of how it will come to pass. Even at the birth of the New Testament church we see that God spoke through the apostle Peter, in Acts 2:

Acts 2:17 NKJV
And it shall come to pass in the last days, says God, That I will pour out My Spirit on all flesh; Your sons and your daughters shall prophesy, your young men shall see visions, your old men shall dream dreams.

This is a powerful promise to the church of today. This is a promise to us right now! We get to live this promise as children of God, and it is speaking to us even now!

The latter part of this verse is what I hope this book helps you understand: "and your young men shall see visions…"

God will give us actual vision just as he did Ananias, (Acts 9:10), Peter (Acts 10:17), Paul as a young man (Acts 22:17 and 26:19) and John, the youngest of the apostles (Revelation 1:10), though he was advanced in years when he saw the visions in the book of Revelation. God will at times pull back the curtain of heaven and give us a glimpse. More often, though, He will use what is already in us or around us, that thing that is deposited in us at some point in time —a deep passion that He uses for His glory when we are yielded to His will, which will be discussed further in chapter four.

"…and your old men shall dream dreams."

I find it interesting that "old men" is specified, because the apostles were relatively young when this was penned in the book of Acts. The inclusive nature of this verse is men, women, old, and young. It is saying that everyone can experience God's Spirit and everything HE has for us! So this isn't an "either/or" promise, it's a "both/and" promise.

Dreams are powerful and they can drive the life of a person if we pursue them. This book is not an exhaustive guide about reaching your dreams by any stretch. It is something that will help propel you to understand the God-given vision and dream He has planned for you since the beginning of time itself. It's interesting that the biblical narrative God had me use for this book was from the life of Joseph, which took place in the book of Genesis – the very first book of the Bible! That means these principles are timeless. They've been around since man started walking the earth, and they are just as relevant today as they were then.

When you close your eyes, what do you see? When you have a free moment to daydream, what is it about? When you think about what will make you most fulfilled, most happy, and more importantly; the most impact for God's kingdom, then I believe you are beginning to dream. When we have a picture of a preferred future in our hearts and minds, it has a lot to do with the dream God has for our life. Dreams that are from God have a lot more to do with His purpose in the earth than our selfish desire. If our dreams center around more money for a nicer car or a bigger boat then we may need to go back to the drawing board and figure out the dream God has for us. If our dream is just about us, then our dream is too small. Every God-given dream will have a foundation of connecting people to God through a relationship with Jesus Christ. That dream will take on many different forms for many different people but if it is a God-given dream, the end result should be the motive of redemption and a love for mankind.

Maybe you don't know Jesus, or this God talk is kinda new to you. Maybe someone handed you this book and you feel a little aimless. Regardless, I believe this book will help you discover God's dream for you, but it all starts with God. It starts with having a relationship with Him through Jesus Christ. Becoming a Christian isn't the end all of reaching your dreams, but I can say with all certainty that it is God's dream for your life. God's dream is to have a relationship with you. It's your time to fulfill God's dream and start a relationship with Him.

You may have said "the sinner's prayer" a billion times, you may have attended a few church services, maybe you have reached a "new state of consciousness," talked with a "spiritual advisor," or grown up in church as a preacher's kid, but none of those things has any validation with God. He wants a relationship with us!

Please understand having a relationship with and faith in Jesus Christ is the only way to achieve salvation and real communion with God.

Applying the principles found within this book, or in the Bible for that matter, will help you in the short-term, but for lasting change and eternal transformation you can never cancel out a thriving relationship with the living God by just receiving His principles and not Him. If this is done, it results in a humanized, secular gospel that has the outward appearance of godliness but in its nature denies the power of Holy Spirit. This will result in a life that looks like the one the Apostle Paul describes in 2 Timothy 3:1-9. Eventually it will lead to folly and foolishness.

If you are at a place where there is absolute uncertainty about your relational standing with God, stop reading this book, pick up a Bible, go to Romans 10:8-11 and simply go to Him in prayer. Ask for Him to come into your life, confess Jesus as your Lord, but more than saying it, believe it. God doesn't care how you pray, at this moment; right now he just wants to hear you speak to Him. Please understand, this is just barely scratching the surface on prayer and what it means to have a relationship with God. There are many resources available to you to learn more about growing as a Christian. I encourage you to discover and devour as much as you can, starting with the Bible. For now though, we need to establish a new connection or a renewed connection to the life-giving power of God that will help you through the process of living your God-given dream. My prayer is that you read and apply this book, implement some daily habits of spiritual growth, and get plugged into a life-giving, Bible-based, Holy Spirit led church. I believe this will help the process further along. From there, my hope is that your relationship with God is more amazing than you could've ever imagined!

CHAPTER 1

The Gift of a Dream

THE MOST WONDERFUL TIME OF YEAR

I love Christmas. It's one of the most wonderful times of the year. It's a time where we get to take time off from work and be with family. It's a time where we get to watch some awesome Christmas movies like, "Elf" and "A Christmas Story." It's a time when we get to eat all the stuff that we've avoided for an entire year. Peanut butter fudge, buckeyes, cookies, brownies…oh my! I can definitely imagine that! It's also a time when we get to give gifts to our loved ones as an act of generosity and as an example of the greatest gift that was ever bestowed upon mankind by an ever-loving God – his name is Jesus. Gift giving is God's nature. One of the most basic scriptures we see at football games on big cardboard signs every Sunday is John 3:16, *"For God so loved the world that he **gave** his one and only Son, that whoever believes in him shall not perish but have eternal life."* God is a good God with good plans. He's a giving God who wants to give not only to Christians but to the world. He loves the world. The entire world; not just the Christian world but everybody, everywhere, for all time and so much that He gave his son Jesus as gift. All we must do is receive the gift of this amazing relationship.

Jesus is the greatest gift anyone could ever receive. I remember when I was an 18 year old, drug-addicted, skinny surfer kid sitting in the back row of a youth church in central Florida and the call of God came on my life. I remember it like it was yesterday. I was watching my youth pastor preach his heart to a generation of young people that were hungry for God and I heard a still small voice, not audibly, but it seemed like it was right in my gut. It said, "You will do that." That was it. Nothing more at that point.

I didn't understand it at first but the only thing I saw was my youth pastor preaching like a man on fire. And I thought, "That?! You've got to be kidding. Me doing that?! No way." But again, it was the Holy Spirit calling me and it was as clear as day, "Yes. That." From there I went through a series of thoughts ranging from disbelief to inspiration. Could I really do that? Could I really be a preacher? Could I really be a pastor? Is there really stuff in me that God wants to use to build His kingdom? The answer was, "Yes." It took a number of years before any of that could take place. I'm still not where I want to be and certainly not where I feel God wants me. At this point in the journey, I'm still experiencing God's blessing, but it all started with a gift.

The first gift I received was the gift of Jesus. Just a few months before that experience with the Holy Spirit in that youth church. I found myself in a world of hurt. At this point in my life I was completely addicted to drugs, selling drugs to support my own habit and was basically homeless; sleeping from couch to couch. There was a time frame of about two weeks where my world came crashing down and it seemed God was ready to activate His purpose on my life. Let me preface this by saying that God doesn't make bad things happen, but I fully believe God will allow the consequences of our actions to get us to a place of utter and total dependence on Him. This two-week time frame was just that.

It started with me being at the wrong place at the wrong time. I grew up around some pretty rough people. I was at a party and was jumped by three guys who had accused me of something I hadn't done. I narrowly escaped before I took anymore bodily harm because I happened to be with friends who stepped in. After getting home and tending to my wounds, I fell asleep. The next morning I woke up to find my car had been broken into and everything was stripped. It didn't stop there, though — within the next day or two my car engine seized up, leaving me without a ride! So now I couldn't deliver drugs or get to either of my fast food jobs I had at the time, which means I had no money to pay rent! When you don't have rent money... you get evicted. Now there I was, beat up, addicted, broken, hurting, and homeless, and because of the string of family relationships I had damaged, I had nowhere to go. It feels like a country song at this point, good thing I didn't have a dog!

Like anybody who's hit rock bottom, you become desperate. I called the only person I could think of who would actually answer my call... my mom. It wasn't an easy conversation. I begged her for a place to stay, and because she knew what I was about and where I was in life, she refused to have me there. I then appealed to her maternal side (which every prodigal son does) and she struck a deal with me. The deal was that I would go to church every Sunday and Wednesday night, get a job, and quit using drugs. Oh gee, that's it? I had faked church my whole life, so this was easy. Little did I know that she had started going to a Spirit-filled church that was unlike any church I'd ever attended. From the first church service, my life was changed. I wasn't perfect and won't be until I meet Jesus face-to-face, but over the next several years my life started to take a drastically different trajectory. I was headed from death to life, from purposelessness to destiny, from mediocrity to greatness.

I had received the gift of salvation in a relationship with Jesus. I was changed forever, but this also meant that I would have to change my goals and my desires. My whole outlook on life needed to be different. I couldn't go back into the same environments or continue with the same relationships. I needed to pursue God and the dreams, destiny, and purpose He had for my life. That was the second gift I received after the gift of salvation: the gift of purpose & destiny. The gift of God's dream for my life. And that was what happened in that youth church back in the day.

CHOICES, CHOICES, AND MORE CHOICES

Living your dream is not always a comfortable choice, it's not the convenient choice, and it's certainly not the clear choice. There are so many choices we can make in life. Safe choices, dangerous choices, boring choices, mundane choices, wise choices, and stupid choices — the choices are endless. The one choice you'll never regret is choosing to pursue God's dream for your life. Choosing to pursue and live your God-given dream is unlike anything else you'll ever do in your life.

I've made a lot of bad choices in my life. Some were as devastating as running a red light and getting into a car accident, and some were as insignificant as a bad order at a restaurant. Regardless of the choice I made, it was mine to make. The amazing thing about God's love — and the slightly scary thing — is that God gives us a choice in the matter. He doesn't just force us to live our dream, but He also doesn't just let our dream fall into our lap either. We have to choose to live our dreams. We have to choose to work hard. We have to choose to be great parents. We have to choose to build that business. We have to choose to be people of integrity. No matter where we come from or where we are on the socioeconomic scale, the one thing that remains the same is that we all have the power of choice. We can choose right now to pursue God's call on our life or we can choose to live in mediocrity. We can choose to make our marriages better or not. We can choose to raise kids God's way or not. We can choose to pursue God's call for us or not. You get the picture. It's up to us.

This type of thinking is liberating from religious and false beliefs. Somehow Christians have gotten into the mentality that if I make some positive faith confessions then God will just "make things happen," even if I just sit on my couch eating potato chips all day. At the other end of the spectrum, believing that if we just work really, really hard and have the mentality, "If it is to be, it's up to me." Unfortunately, this mentality cancels out the opportunity to see the supernatural power of God at work in our lives to make the dream happen, because we are depending on us and only us. The reality is that a God-given dream is always a partnership between us and God. There is a rhythm of life that God wants for us.

Matthew 11:28 MSG
Are you tired? Worn out? Burned out on religion? Come to me. Get away with me and you'll recover your life. I'll show you how to take a real rest. Walk with me and work with me—watch how I do it. Learn the unforced rhythms of grace. I won't lay anything heavy or ill-fitting on you. Keep company with me and you'll learn to live freely and lightly.

> **WE DO WHAT ONLY WE CAN DO THEN GOD DOES WHAT ONLY GOD CAN DO.**

We do the natural work of working hard, staying faithful, and remaining humble, and God does the supernatural work of blessing us with the reality of living His dream for our life. Let me explain it like this: God can't go the gym for us, that's our job. God can't make phone calls for us, that's our job. God can't tithe for us, that's our job. God can't invest for the future for us, that's our job. What God does is keep us in supernatural health when we choose to take care of ourselves. God can give us favor when no amount of schmoozing will work. God will open the windows of heaven on our lives when we tithe. God can make things happen when we do the things that we are supposed to do. God does what he does when we do what we are supposed to do.

NICE COAT YA GOT THERE

I love the story of Joseph — there's drama, betrayal, assumptions…it's kinda like a worship team fighting over skinny jeans! Seriously though, Hollywood couldn't script a better drama or reality show! (Yes, reality shows are scripted, sorry to burst your bubble.) Anyway, the life of Joseph has so many lessons. Throughout this book we will discover many identifiable principles you can discover from this amazing account.

Genesis 37:1-4 NJKV
Now Jacob dwelt in the land where his father was a stranger, in the land of Canaan. This is the history of Jacob. Joseph, being seventeen years old, was feeding the flock with his brothers. And the lad was with the sons of Bilhah and the sons of Zilpah, his father's wives; and Joseph brought a bad report of them to his father. Now Israel loved Joseph more than all his children, because he was the son of his old age. Also he made him a tunic of many colors. But when his brothers saw that their father loved him more than all his brothers, they hated him and could not speak peaceably to him.

As a young man, Joseph was the most favorite child. He was also the youngest child, which had its own disadvantages in the culture in which he was raised. As the youngest child,

Joseph wouldn't receive near the inheritance or favor that the oldest son would receive when Jacob passed away.

This is an interesting exception though, because for some reason God favored Joseph with his father Jacob. The Bible isn't clear on this point, but my belief is that Jacob was informed by the Spirit of God that Joseph was special. The verse says, *"because he was the son of his old age,"* meaning that he could've been Jacob's last son because he was up in years. So Jacob was looking at Joseph as a promise of hope and legacy.

As the favored child, Joseph received a special gift from his father. The scripture says it was a tunic, which is what we would regard as a coat or robe. The coat represented a special relationship to Jacob that the other brothers did not have. We aren't told what the coat was made of. A coat of many colors in that time could have been exotic fabrics from different locales or furs from different animals, but in any of those cases it was of immense value. The interesting thing is this gift was given to Joseph not as a payment or anything that he had earned. It was a gift of favor. This is something we need to understand about God. He will give us a gift and favor us not because we earn it or because we are deserving of it. When God does favor us it's because of His grace. It's because of Jesus. Because of the price Jesus paid on the cross, we will always have a balance of favor with God. We also have favor with men granted by God, but that favor is something we can lose or increase depending on how we steward that relationship.

The scripture says, "But when his brothers saw that their father loved him more than all his brothers, they hated him and could not speak peaceably to him." Favor can be lost with some because of the favor you have with others. Joseph didn't have favor with his brothers because of the favor his father had shown him.

His brothers were what we commonly know as "haters." Like the saying goes, "Haters gonna hate!" and this was true with Joseph because of the jealousy his brothers had for him. Another interesting thing about favor is that God gives it to us when we are going to need it. Favor is not just for a parking spot up front, it is because you are going to really need it! The Bible says "favor surrounds us like a shield" (Psalm 5:12) – well, you only need a shield when you are in a war! Favor is what will help you not just survive but thrive when conditions are at their worst.

The sad thing is that when God favors you, not everyone is going to be happy about it. Not everyone is going to rejoice with you about your gift or your dream. As a matter of fact, most people will be envious. It takes a rare few people to rejoice with you when God blesses you. It takes a selfless mentality to rejoice with others and the blessing God gives them and not you. Joseph's brothers couldn't speak peaceably to him. They couldn't even be cordial to him as their own brother, because jealousy ate them up. It's the same with you. People will be so jealous and envious of God's gift and dream on your life that they won't even be able to speak peaceably to you. They might even actually speak badly about you on a public platform because you are moving forward with the dream God gave you. Regardless though, your job is to build the dream not defend yourself!

You must understand this if you want to see your dream come to pass: **it does not matter what anyone says about you or your dream.** The only thing that matters is what God has said and what you say. Don't you dare agree with people who are speaking death over your dream. Now on the other hand if these are people that have your back, don't be foolish! Proverbs 11:14 says, *"Where there is no counsel, the people fall; But in the multitude of counselors there is safety."* So getting advice from godly people filled with wisdom is imperative. But if God has called you to start a business, then start a business. If He has called you to write a song or a book, then write it! If God has called you to plant a church or start a ministry then do it! Whatever God is calling you to do is something that He will find you able to do. It doesn't matter what people say about you or what their opinion is of you, because they didn't call you or gift you with the dream – only God did!

Brilliant men and women throughout history have looked past the doubters and continued on with the dream in their hearts. Walt Disney was one of the great dreamers of our day. Walt created Mickey Mouse in 1928 and was constantly ridiculed for the idea, but he didn't stop. More characters came and eventually more avenues came for the creativity of Disney to be expressed. After Disneyland became a reality in Anaheim, California, Walt wanted to move forward with his biggest feat yet, The Walt Disney World Resort and The Magic Kingdom. Walt was on the hunt for financing this extraordinary idea, but he couldn't land any banker who'd be willing to risk so much money on such a wild dream. In fact, 302 different sources of financing turned Walt down and rejected his dream. Big dreams take big risks, and sometimes you have to surround yourself with people who are a little bit crazy in order to see it come to pass.

Eventually Walt did get the financing he was looking for, and in 1971 the resort that was once a pipe-dream actually became reality. Unfortunately the dreamer died in 1965. On opening day of Disney World, an executive was in conversation with Roy Disney, Walt's younger brother. After they had made a bit of small talk, the executive turned to him and with complete honor in his eyes and heart he said, "Wow, if Walt could've seen this day!" It's fabled that Roy turned back to the man and with a rarely stern face, looked him right in the eyes and said, "He did." It's obvious what Roy meant. He meant dreamers see things others don't long before they are reality. As a dreamer God will give you a unique vision, but it's up to you to have the tenacity to keep moving forward with the dream.

SHUT YO MOUTH SUCKA!

Genesis 37:5-8 NKJV
Now Joseph had a dream, and he told it to his brothers; and they hated him even more. So he said to them, "Please hear this dream which I have dreamed: There we were, binding sheaves in the field. Then behold, my sheaf arose and also stood upright; and indeed your sheaves stood all around and bowed down to my sheaf." And his brothers said to him, "Shall you indeed reign over us? Or shall you indeed have dominion over us?" So they hated him even more for his dreams and for his words.

The first thing about having a great dream: keep your mouth shut about it, at first. The moment you open your mouth you better be absolutely sure that you are ready to move forward with it regardless of what people say. Because people, even those closest to you, will eventually hate you because of your dream. I've found that when people don't have a dream of their own they end up attacking those who do. I've also found that when people have their own dream and yours happens to be bigger or greater than theirs, somehow they will attack you out of insecurity and intimidation. Having a dream can intimidate some and inspire others. We must use wisdom and discernment sharing our dream with the right people at the right time in order to get the right outcome.

Dreams take time and there is usually a long winding road to get there. Don't brag about seeing something that hasn't happened yet! Joseph's brothers hated him for sharing his dream. A wise mentor of mine once told me that I "needed to keep my counsel to myself." He was telling me this out of love because I have a tendency to get really excited about something God has revealed to me or something great that He has done in me or maybe an idea that could be a huge financial engine and I immediately want to share with others. The problem is people are rarely as excited to hear it as I am to share it. The best thing we can do is to keep it to ourselves until the right time being in the right environment with the right people.

This happened to Mary when she was told that she would be pregnant with Jesus. We see it all throughout the beginning of the book of Luke. Chapters one and two God used angels, shepherds, and others to speak to her about God's dream for her life. God's dream was to find someone he could use in order to birth the Savior of the world. When Mary was chosen there was an overwhelming sense of joy but with it came an ultimate responsibility because she was birthing the One who would save humanity. Did you think Mary had a little something to tell those close to her? She was birthing the Son of God! I mean c'mon if anybody had some tea to spill, it was Mary. She was Jesus' mom! Hello?! But she didn't say a word, except to a few close friends who believed her and loved her. Mary knew the importance of what she was carrying and she also knew that she needed to keep it quiet!

Luke 2:19 NIV
But Mary treasured up all these things and pondered them in her heart.

I love how The Message translation says it:

Mary kept all these things to herself, holding them dear, deep within herself.

Sometimes we will have a dream for years and never tell it to anybody, and that's ok. I'd much rather hold on to a dream silently for years than share it with the wrong person and have them get all negative about it straight away and speak death over it! Sometimes the only person you can tell about your dream is you. There will be times in your life when the bottom falls out, the marriage falls apart, the kids you raised hardly talk to you anymore, the business fails, or any other tragedy takes place...in those times your dream might be all you have to hang on to. Ultimately our lifeline is Jesus. He wants us to hang on to Him with everything we have in us. But I believe that He places the dream inside of us to give us something to live for, something to look forward to. The dream can help get us through some of the darkest times of our lives. When we don't know what to do or how it's all going to turn out, the dream is the light at the end of the tunnel. Keeping the dream deep in our hearts is vital to living the life God intended for us!

Genesis 37:9-11 NKJV
Then he had another dream, and he told it to his brothers. "Listen," he said, "I had another dream, and this time the sun and moon and eleven stars were bowing down to me." When he told his father as well as his brothers, his father rebuked him and said, "What is this dream you had? Will your mother and I and your brothers actually come

and bow down to the ground before you?" His brothers were jealous of him, but his father kept the matter in mind.

Here we go again. Joseph didn't get the hint that his brothers didn't want to hear about the dream God had given him. He seemed to be a little stubborn or thick-headed, which is pretty common with dreamers. That's actually a good thing, because you have to believe in the dream even when no one else does. But learning to keep your mouth shut and your heart open is something we have to do when we have a big dream. This was a lesson that Joseph was going to learn the hard way. Sometimes we have to learn the hard way too, but if we understand this principle it will save us a lot of heartache, pain, and rejection. I've found that if we share our dream with people who don't like us or don't care for our dream it creates a wall and eventually could result in creating some enemies!

It's interesting that Joseph's father got angry with him and rebuked him as well. This is the guy that gave Joseph so much favor remember? This is the guy that gave Joseph his coat of many colors. This is also the guy that is rebuking Joseph for sharing his dream with people that could care less. Sometimes God will bring people into your life who will help guide you in your dream, but you must be humble enough to accept their direction and correction. The last part of the passage of scripture says *"his father kept the matter in mind."* This is interesting because Jacob didn't dismiss the dream Joseph had. He may have actually believed it, if he was to be honest – he just didn't like it and that's ok, not everyone will like your vision even those that love you. Those you have favor with might believe in your dream, but you must be willing to prove faithful. When you prove yourself faithful in the little things with those who are familiar with you, then they will believe you when you share the dream. Jacob probably knew deep in his heart that Joseph's dream was real, but the timing in which it was shared was out of line.

Timing is an important factor when it comes to your dream. Throughout this book, the timing of a dream will be mentioned. When God reveals a dream to us, most likely it is years off for us. If we get impatient with the dream and the fulfillment of it, we can actually postpone the dream if we rush through the process. The process of a dream and the preparation of the dreamer work hand in hand.

BEWARE OF THE DREAM KILLERS

Genesis 37:18-20 NKJV
Now when they saw him afar off, even before he came near them, they conspired against him to kill him. Then they said to one another, "Look, this dreamer is coming! Come therefore, let us now kill him and cast him into some pit; and we shall say, 'Some wild beast has devoured him.' We shall see what will become of his dreams!"

> **DREAMS DON'T DIE, ONLY DREAMERS DO.**

God has given people dreams throughout centuries and these dreams have lasted far beyond the lifespan of the dreamer. Our dream should be something that is made up of legacy and something that the generations after us can carry. This is why it is so important to guard the dream God has given you fiercely! Be on alert: You will encounter dream killers! These are people who want to kill God's dream for us. Maybe they don't want to kill us physically, but they would love nothing more than for us to stay out of destiny and apart from our dream. Sometimes it's even unintentional, just because all someone has ever known is to pull others down. It could also be birthed out of an injury or hurt that comes from their own life. Maybe you caused it, or maybe you simply remind them of someone who did. Regardless of whatever it is that bugs them about you, it's their issue and not yours! The interesting thing about dream killers is that they are actually doing you a favor when they come against you. The more junk they try to throw in your way is more material God is given to work with. Remember, people can't control your destiny. If you are submitted to God, He will use whatever circumstance in your life to drive you towards the destiny and purpose He has in mind for you.

Romans 8:28 NKJV
And we know that all things work together for good to those who love God, to those who are the called according to His purpose.

If you are a child of God, you are called according to His purpose for your life. Everything isn't going to come up roses and not everything is going to work out like you imagined, but God will use everything to work for your good. God has the best intentions for you at all times. There will be people who have good intentions, but they aren't like God's intentions for you. No matter what hits your life, it has to be filtered through the loving hands of your heavenly Father. He has your best intentions at heart. Dream killers may actually be a part of God's provisional plan on your life. God has a perfect plan, and then He has many provisional plans, regardless of how many bad choices we make. He is the God of infinite plans and He is the God of infinite chances. Our choices and the consequences built within may postpone our destiny, but we have to trust in our Father in heaven that He has many opportunities awaiting us. These dream killers, these people are actually doing you a favor! It's God's dream for you. They can't kill His dream, although they can kill you. They can kill your fervor for the Lord if you allow it. They can kill your attitude if you allow it. They can kill your morale if you allow it. The dream may still be alive but are you? We have to be fully alive and living the dream God has for our lives regardless of what anyone says or does!

I love the last part of the passage in Genesis that says, *"We shall see what will become of his dreams!"* This phrase was actually supposed to be an insult to Joseph and his dream, but it was actually fuel to help propel Joseph onto the next phase of God's dream for his life. This phrase should be rocket fuel for your soul! When someone doubts you say, *"We shall see what will become of my dream!"* When someone hates on you, you should say, *"We shall see what will become of my dream!"* When people try to destroy your character and discredit the gift of God on your life, you should say, "We shall see what will become of my dream!" Make that your confession today!

Say it loud and proud!

> **"WE SHALL SEE WHAT WILL BECOME OF MY DREAM!"**

CHAPTER 2

Dream Deficiency Syndrome

Genesis 39:1-6 NKJV

Now Joseph had been taken down to Egypt. And Potiphar, an officer of Pharaoh, captain of the guard, an Egyptian, bought him from the Ishmaelites who had taken him down there. The Lord was with Joseph, and he was a successful man; and he was in the house of his master the Egyptian. And his master saw that the Lord was with him and that the Lord made all he did to prosper in his hand. So Joseph found favor in his sight, and served him. Then he made him overseer of his house, and all that he had he put under his authority. So it was, from the time that he had made him overseer of his house and all that he had, that the Lord blessed the Egyptian's house for Joseph's sake; and the blessing of the Lord was on all that he had in the house and in the field. Thus he left all that he had in Joseph's hand, and he did not know what he had except for the bread which he ate.

Throughout the story of Joseph we find a young man with a big dream and many inconvenient and painful situations that would seem to work to the contrary of his dream. In the passage above we see that Joseph is in a place he doesn't want to be. He is a slave in Egypt. He is under the actual ownership of another human being. His is not his own at this point. He's in a job he doesn't want to be in, working for a man who, technically, owns his very life. The Bible isn't clear if Joseph complained or if he murmured in his heart, but I would venture to say he was happy to be alive considering his brothers planned to kill him! It's interesting to note the very next verse in this passage talks about the Lord being with Joseph. No matter what we go through, God is with us. Regardless of circumstance, God is with us. Not only was He with Joseph, but His favor was on Joseph so much that his master saw the blessing of the Lord on his life. God will place us in an environment that will help prepare us for destiny. Unfortunately the environment might be a dull, mundane, everyday, day in and day out existence. Regardless of how it feels, God will bless us in that environment.

Romans 8:28 NKJV
And we know that all things work together for good to those who love God, to those who are the called according to His purpose.

I know I keep mentioning this scripture but it bears reminding. Everything, I mean every job, situation, relationship, circumstance; absolutely everything we go through is preparation for the dream God has put in our hearts.

I take the time to think about how throughout my life of ministry, God was preparing me for the call that was specifically on my life. I remember it like it was yesterday. I was sitting in my office as a youth pastor of a mid-size church and we were on a "spending freeze" meaning no one could even buy a pen without proper approval! So as a youth pastor, it meant I had to get creative. We didn't have the budget to hire a graphic designer so I started working in Photoshop more and more. I ended up creating a cool looking little handout for a youth event coming up. I printed it on our color copier on card stock and even cut them myself in our work room at the church. So as the event approached, my pastor came in with a furrowed brow and a serious look on his face wanting to know who I hired to get these cards designed and printed. When I told him I did it, his entire demeanor changed. He changed his tune pretty quick and asked me if I could design his next sermon series for him. I said, "Yes." From there I designed a ton of projects for the church and his ministry, which eventually birthed a business of my own which has been amazing! Here we are years later and

I've designed and consulted for some of the largest ministries in the world, all because I was in a position to say, "Yes." God has used this gift on my life to help ministries go further than ever before and has helped me grow personally and financially! This is how God works. He uses everything for our good and His glory. You may look around at your current circumstance and get frustrated because you feel like God has let you down. The facts are God hasn't let you down. You may be there because it's your next phase of training for your dream and your destiny.

Joseph was to be the leader of a nation. The lessons he learned about authority in Potiphar's house were invaluable. If he would have gotten into pride and arrogance thinking he was too good for this environment, there was a possibility he could have been killed. It was vital to Joseph's destiny and dream for him to learn the lesson that God had for him in while he was in Potiphar's house. I want to encourage you right now; God has you where you are for a reason. He may not have placed you there but you are where you are and ultimately you must trust that it is for our good and God's glory.

Do not give up on where you are in life! This is the time to get fired up and determined that you won't quit! As the scripture indicates, if you are called of God to live His dream for your life then all things, every little thing, you experience will work for your good and His glory.

THE DIVINE LOTTERY TICKET

Most people miss the blessing of everyday life because they are waiting for the "The Big One" to happen – the big day, the big promotion, the big opportunity, the big relationship.

The problem is "The Big One" will probably never happen because a dream is built by individual steps day in and day out. Most people have a "lottery ticket" mentality. You can't win the lottery unless you play. The most probable outcome though is you probably won't win even if you do play! I know that sounds discouraging from a book that is supposed to be encouraging but we must understand that God doesn't work on a "lottery ticket" mentality, He works on a savings and accrual mentality. When we have a savings account, whether it's a 401k or mutual fund or whatever, we receive an accrual of interest and over time the fund grows because of our constant attention and dedication to it. It's the same thing with our dream. "The Big One" doesn't just happen, it takes a daily, constant attention in order for it to come to pass.

In geology, we have been taught that water has the ability to shape rocks and boulders. If we were to take a cup of water, walk outside and pour it on a rock, well...we'd have a wet rock. In contrast, if we were to see this same thing happen over a period of 10 years, 20 years, maybe even 100 years, then we would see that rock shaped by the constant pouring of water. The power isn't in the water, the power is in the consistency. The consistency day in and day out is what God requires of us and what our dream requires of us. It's the ability to keep doing the right things over and over again. Notice I said the "right" things. A short definition of insanity is doing the same thing over and over and expecting different results. When we do the right things over and over and get results, then we keep doing them. Once those results diminish, we don't quit, we just change the tactic and approach to what we are doing. We become obsessive when it comes to tweaking our strategy. This is what it takes! The end result is what we are after, not how we got there. Back to the analogy of geology, water takes many different forms in order to shape the earth accordingly. Sometimes it becomes hard and rock-solid through ice-cold glaciers, sometimes it is heated by the earth's core and comes up boiling hot through springs, but whatever form it takes, it's still water and the end result is our earth has been shaped by the power of consistency.

The laws of God don't change when it comes to our life. The same law of consistency applies to our life and the life of our dream. We must keep moving forward, keep pressing into God and His word, keep doing daily things to see our dream come to pass. The problem we get into is that we compare our "behind-the-scenes" to someone else's "highlight reel!" We didn't see Michael Jordan shoot hoops everyday for hours on end. All we saw was him on the court being the best basketball player the game has ever seen. In order to become what God has called us to become, we need to stay faithful behind the scenes. There will be a day when we are out in front of everybody and there will be a highlight reel shown. The sad thing is most people live for the highlight reel instead of the character building behind-the-scenes. The pain you go through behind-the-scenes, the haters you ignore behind-the-scenes, the critics you overcome behind-the-scenes, the voices you silence behind-the-scenes. Notice I said, "behind-the-scenes" every time. We aren't here to confront, we're here to love. God is your Defender. You don't need to voice yourself publicly. Those "behind-the-scenes" moments are what bring weight to your voice. When people look at your highlight reel there will be an intangible weight they feel, not because of the highlight reel but because of the "behind-the-scenes" moments it took to create the reel itself. You haven't gone through what you've gone through for no reason! God is going to use your mess! God loves taking those who would be counted as least and using them in the greatest of ways.

DDS - DREAM DEFICIENCY SYNDROME

I've done some extensive research on a common syndrome that plagues a lot of people throughout the world, called "immunodeficiency." Better known as immune deficiency syndrome (IDS). It is a state in which the immune system's ability to fight infectious disease is compromised or entirely absent. There are many types of IDS but regardless of the name, this is a terrible thing to have. From how it's been described, it isn't like having a full-blown disease that lays you up in the hospital somewhere, but at the same time it isn't being fully well either. It's said to be somewhere in the middle because you can't operate at full capacity. Your body is constantly fighting something off, which affects how you feel. There are treatments that help with this disorder, but many people who have it will tell you that they feel like they've missed out on the fullness of their life because of it. Many people, on the other hand, have overcome how they feel with natural or medicinal treatments and although they may have been diagnosed with this syndrome, they are truly living life to the fullest of their God-given ability.

Like IDS, there is another syndrome that may not kill you, but will leave you in a state of mediocrity. I actually made it up. But please, humor me. *Dream Deficiency Syndrome* is made up of symptoms that will keep a person from their God-given dream. As a matter of fact, DDS is something that people can be healed of. The healing comes through how we approach our life and more specifically, how we approach our dream. Many people miss out the fullness of God's dream for their life because they allow the symptoms of DDS to overwhelm them. God wants us to live a full size dream! It's usually a state of mind, thought process, or an attitude. I've compiled a list of symptoms and how we can overcome them!

SYMPTOMS OF DDS

- **Mediocrity is a symptom of DDS**

It seems the older we get the more mediocre things can become. As we move forward in life just by sheer age alone we can start to settle for what is, rather than dreaming about what could be. The kids grow up and we're ok with that. The mortgage gets paid and all is well. The job gets stale but at least we're employed. Things just remain in a rut.

We even begin to settle in the way we do things. We adopt the philosophy, "Well good enough for government work!" Things just become average, mundane, boring. Our relationship with our spouse begins to deteriorate because we allow other mediocre things to come in and take its place, and in turn the closest relationship we have on earth becomes routine. How did all this happen? How did things become so blah?

We stopped dreaming.

> **THE MOMENT WE STOP DREAMING IS THE MOMENT WE START DYING.**

Dreams have a tendency to challenge us in our thinking. They have a tendency to motivate us to be more excellent, to say that "good enough isn't good enough." In order for us to live our dream we have to move from mediocrity to excellence. We are called to strive for excellence. There's another story of a young man named Daniel. We don't have time to jump into all of his story but Daniel was an extraordinary young man who was brought in as a slave. Although he was considered a spoil of war, Daniel did everything with excellence. He and his friends were handsome, intelligent young men who had the hand of God on their life. The scripture says Daniel exemplified this spirit during his service as a highly regarded administrator in a secular environment. It says that "he distinguished himself among the administrators . . . because of his exceptional qualities" so much so that "they could find no corruption in him, because he was trustworthy and neither corrupt nor negligent" (Daniel 6:3-4). Excellence does not necessarily mean the absence of mistakes, but it does mean the presence of faith and determination. To be excellent at whatever God has called you to do, you must first ask for His strength to accomplish the task and then, secondly, His endurance to complete it. Daniel was met with obstacles in his endeavor to serve the Lord wholeheartedly, but he remained steadfast to the course of action he believed the Lord set for him to take.

You must also recognize that there is a difference between striving to be perfect versus endeavoring to be excellent. Achieving perfection is an impossible task because it never makes allowances for errors or missteps. Consequently, condemnation and discouragement often follow one's pursuit of perfection, because these unrealistic expectations lead to feelings of worthlessness and a sense of inadequacy. A person who strives for excellence doesn't give up when he makes mistakes, and he doesn't avoid tasks for fear of failure. The true goal of excellence is to do the best you can with what you have at every moment. Andrew Carnegie said, "An average person puts only 25% of their energy and ability into their work. The world takes its hat off to those who put more than 50% capacity in, and stands on its head to those few and far between souls who devote 100%." Excellence isn't having the best or the most expensive solution.

> **EXCELLENCE IS SIMPLY DOING THE BEST WITH WHAT GOD HAS ENTRUSTED TO YOU.**

Our God is an excellent God and He has set the standard fo us.

Psalm 8:1 NKJV
O Lord, our Lord, How excellent is Your name in all the earth, Who have set Your glory above the heavens!

- **Regret is a symptom of DDS**

Regret is when we spend more time talking about what should've been rather than what could be. A major symptom of DDS is when our vision is for today and yesterday rather than tomorrow. We must overcome regret in order for us to live our dreams. I think everyone deals with it at some level.

Every morning I wake up, it seems like I hear a bell go off in my head. Not a dinner bell or a little reminder sound on my phone, it sounds like a fight bell. It feels like I'm in the cage with a 500lb. gorilla... and his name is REGRET. It's tattooed across his chest. He's a beast, a scary beast that would eat most people for breakfast. Sometimes I wake up and he's on my chest, just sitting there beating up my heart with feelings of past mistakes. Sometimes he's pouncing on my noggin bombarding me with thoughts of the past. Regardless of where he is, I know I have one of two choices, fight or get beat up. So, every morning I choose to fight.

I love what Romans 8:1 says: "Therefore, there is now no condemnation for those who are in Christ Jesus." This verse is a great reminder that I don't have to deal with regret or allow it to get the best part of my day. Do I regret stuff? Of course. I regret the dumb little things I do and I regret the major things I've done that have hurt my family and friends. The thing about all this is... I'm forgiven. I'm forgiven by God and for the most part, I'm forgiven by people. Regret can eat up a lot of our lives if we allow it. That's right, allow it. It's a choice. I'm not going to live my life in the past and you don't need to either. The past is just that, the past. We can't change it, we can't heal it, we can't do anything about it except forget it. So let's live today the best we can and it will help insure a better tomorrow. Leave the past in the past.

> **AS LONG AS WE LIVE IN THE PAST WE ARE DEAD TO OUR FUTURE.**

I'm not a massive fan of zombies but they are such an interesting concept and I know I'll irritate some religious people with this illustration but... eh. Anyway, when we live in the past we are the walking dead in our future. We are like zombies just walking through life with no vision, no foresight, no true brain activity because we are stuck. Stuck in a moment. Stuck in a hurt. Stuck in a betrayal. Stuck in bitterness, anger, revenge. Listen – you can't move forward, truly move forward, until you release the people who hurt you and the past that wants to keep you captive.

Why don't we release? Why don't we let go of hurts and the past? I believe it's fear. We fear what the future might hold for us. The fear of the unknown paralyzes us if we let it. We'd rather stay in the comfort of our pain because we don't know what the healing will look like. We must trust God. More specifically, the process of God. If He is truly sovereign and He is truly crazy in love with us, then we must trust that we are right where we are for a reason.

It's time to forget the past and move forward into our destiny. Our great God has a purpose and destiny that is specific for us. The only thing that will hold us back is our past if we choose to live there.

Philippians 3:13 NKJV
Brethren, I do not count myself to have apprehended; but one thing I do, forgetting those things which are behind and reaching forward to those things which are ahead,

- **Escapism is a symptom of DDS**

The term "escapism" is reserved for those who take excessive time away from real life to the point that they seem to be trying to escape from it. Traditionally regarded as extreme, escapism is in fact increasingly the norm for many people. Escapism is not defined by the behavior itself but the motivation behind it. People get so depressed about their own lives that they'd rather watch reality TV than live their own reality. Some take it to the extreme and start to use drugs and alcohol to help them break from reality. They become numb to their own circumstance so that they don't have to face the weight of living the life God has intended for them. I did say weight. Our destiny is a weight and a burden that God has made us responsible for. We can't get too stressed out about it though. Even Jesus said in Matthew 11:30, *"For my yoke is easy and my burden is light."* Notice he didn't say there wasn't a yoke or a burden. We must take responsibility with our lives and how we spend our time. In America, we've been drilled with marketing phrases like, "You deserve a break today." The problem is we think we're entitled to live on break… always. I'm all for vacations, days off, and sabbaticals but we can't allow escapism to become an everyday part of our life.

We have all been built with a "fight or flight" mentality. Escapism is part of that. When things get tough, we just want to get away. Sometimes we should so we don't make a bad decision out of stress, anxiety, or fear, but if we are always escaping and never facing our problems or rising to the challenge our dream may present, then we will never live our dream – only watch people on television live theirs. I don't know about you but I'm over watching people on TV live their dreams. The people on TV aren't watching you live your dream! I'd say it's about time to stop watching them live theirs!

- **Ungratefulness is a symptom of DDS**

Gratitude is the highest form of prayer. Every word we speak is either a prayer of thankfulness or a grumble against God's blessing in our life. An attitude of gratitude is one that God smiles on!Ungratefulness is when we complain about what we don't have rather than be grateful for what we do have.

There's an interesting study that's been done in recent years by CARE International about global wealth. I've found these results at globalrichlist.com. It's a great website that really helps put things in perspective. I was just playing around with some numbers. Check this out, if you make $19,200 dollars a year, which is $10 an hour at 40 hours a week, that puts you in the top 4% income earners in the world! Hopefully that puts a little perspective on our life. I know, I know... here come the justifications. My standard of living is higher or I live in California or I have more kids to feed. I empathize with your situation. For sure, I've been in extremely dire financial straits in my life before but honestly, none of that matters when it comes to gratefulness. Being thankful for what we have honors God. It isn't just saying a prayer of thanks at our meal but living with an attitude of thankfulness and gratitude. Even the principle of the tithe is an exercise in thankfulness. The tithe is when we give the first 10% of our income back to God via the local church. I'm a big believer in the tithe and I've seen it have supernatural results when I give. The tithe is basically a huge "YES" to God. It's putting Him as the owner in our life and putting us in the role of stewards or managers of what He's entrusted to us.

I remember my dad giving me my first brand new skateboard as a kid. I was probably about 11 or 12 years old, and for my birthday he went out and let me pick my first real skateboard. A Lance Mountain Powell Peralta deck with Tracker trucks and Santa Cruz wheels! I have fond memories of that board for sure. One thing my buddies and I used to do was stack our boards sideways to see who could ollie the highest stack of boards. I remember my friend Wayne ollying my board in my driveway and my dad walking out seeing this. He freaked out. I didn't see anything wrong with it because it's just what we did, but my dad took it as a sign of disrespect. He didn't realize that we buy boards and they get banged up. It's just part of skating. He didn't feel I was being a good steward of what he had entrusted to me. I learned a good lesson on stewardship that day. It's kind of a silly story but it's the same with God. He entrusts to us time and money everyday and sometimes I wonder if He is up in heaven freaking out because we aren't stewarding what He's given us properly. I'm sure He's not…but I think it would be wise for us to thank Him and live life with an attitude of gratitude. If we are ungrateful on the journey to our dream, it's unlikely that we will actually live our dream or enjoy living our dream. I look at gratefulness as an elevator to the next level.

> **GRATEFULNESS IS AN ELEVATOR TO THE NEXT LEVEL.**

When we step in the elevator we a have a choice of buttons to push. We can push the "grumble" button and go down a level or we can push the "thank you" button and go up a level. The more we push the "thank you" button the higher we go, because God can trust us with His blessing in our life. This symptom of ungratefulness is a huge hindrance to living our dream. We must choose to be thankful for what we have.

- **Comparison is a symptom of DDS**

Comparison has the ability to keep us focused on someone else's dream and life rather than our own. Like I mentioned earlier, you end up comparing your behind-the-scenes with other people's highlight reels. We didn't see the hours and hours Michael Jordan practiced on the court, but we did see the six NBA championships he earned. The thing about comparison is; it isn't real. It doesn't make any sense to compare our lives to someone else's because they have had a completely different life experience than us. We didn't see the things they had to go through in order for them to have the success they have today. Until you know their story you may not want their glory! Maybe we just see the big building or nice house, but we didn't see the years of pain, labor, and hard work it took to get to that place. It's crazy to compare a 60-year-old who has made smart investments his whole life to an 18-year-old who hasn't had nearly the amount of earning time. The comparison just doesn't make any sense! We have to stay in our own lane when it comes to comparison. The only person we should be comparing ourselves to… is ourselves!

- **Are you more loving than you were the same time last year?**

- **Are you more generous than you were the same time last year?**

- **Do you have more integrity than you did the same time last year?**

- **Have you grown more emotionally and relationally than the same time last year?**

- **Are you earning more income than you did the same time last year?**

These are the questions we should be asking. Looking to other models of success is fine, but when we get into comparison it is deadly to our own dream, because it is our dream. Those people are living their own dreams and we are called to live ours! Comparison with others goes far back as when humans were created, I'm sure. Even Jesus dealt with comparison in his own disciples. Let's look at this exchange found in the book of John.

John 21:18-22 NKJV
And after saying this he said to him, "Follow me." Peter turned and saw the disciple whom Jesus loved following them, the one who had been reclining at table close to him and had said, "Lord, who is it that is going to betray you?" When Peter saw him, he said to Jesus, "Lord, what about this man?" Jesus said to him, "If it is my will that he remain until I come, what is that to you? You follow me!"

Wow! Jesus got tough with Peter on this one! If Jesus wanted him to stay immortal then what's it to you!? I love Jesus, He makes it so plain. Jesus basically laid the foundation of what we are supposed to do with a God-given dream. We follow Him. We seek Him and we serve Him. Our dream should revolve around us helping people in the name of Jesus. We don't ask why someone else is succeeding as if God is picking favorites. We're all His favorite!

We crave to know how we stack up in comparison to others. God will not judge me according to my superiority or inferiority. This isn't the standard by which anything is measured. Jesus has a work for me to do and a completely different or similar one for you to do. It is not what he has given anyone else to do.

> **STOP COMPARING YOURSELF TO OTHERS, THEY JUST DON'T MEASURE UP TO YOU.**

- **Laziness is a symptom of DDS**

Being a self-starter is a major key in order to live your God-given dream. God gives us the dream and the vision for our future but it's up to us to do the work to get it done. Laziness is when our intentions are stronger than our actions and our execution is weak in comparison to our dream. The only time success comes before work is in the dictionary! We have to be willing to work hard in order for our dream to come to pass. Businesses don't build themselves. Churches don't grow themselves. Songs and books don't write themselves. There is always a leader that must take hold of the dream God has given them and run with it!

2 Thessalonians 3:10-12 NASB
For even when we were with you, we used to give you this order: if anyone is not willing to work, then he is not to eat, either. For we hear that some among you are leading an undisciplined life, doing no work at all, but acting like busybodies. Now such persons we command and exhort in the Lord Jesus Christ to work in quiet fashion and eat their own bread.

Proverbs 10:4 NASB
Poor is he who works with a negligent hand, But the hand of the diligent makes rich.

Proverbs 13:4 NASB
The soul of the sluggard craves and gets nothing, But the soul of the diligent is made fat.

I look at our dream as a partnership with God. If we do the natural work we are supposed to do then God does the supernatural work that only HE can do. We cannot allow ourselves to become sluggish and lazy when it comes to our dream. We should be taking daily steps, no matter how small, in order to reach our dream.

- **Status Quo is a symptom of DDS**

Living in status quo is so subtle, but ultimately deadly to our dream. Status quo is a place where we just settle in a daily, weekly, monthly, and eventually an annual routine. The problem is our daily routine becomes one of maintenance rather than growth. Routine can be great but it's what is accomplished in those routines that matter. Status quo is when the same routine is done but no results come forth from the activity. Status quo has a level of comfort to it that makes us feel safe. Whenever we initiate change we initiate risk. Risk isn't something people like.

Status quo tells people what to do instead of how to think or who to be. It has a feeling of conformity. Instead of empowering you to change, it keeps you locked in maintenance mode so that growth is never even an option. When we look to the future, we will find that status quo gets left behind. What's interesting and sad is that when we start to make changes in our life and gear up towards living our dream, not everybody will be excited about it. People will come out of the woodwork to say you are crazy, and some will even go as far as trying to stop you. I call them the "Warriors of Status Quo." These are the people that will seemingly battle you whenever the suggestion of change comes up. We must understand that we are not battling these people, we are battling status quo itself. These people are fine with the way things are and that's ok for them. For you though, well...for you it's not ok because you are called to greatness. You may have to love some folks from a distance in order for you to reach your dreams and live your destiny.

- **Negativity is a symptom of DDS**

For most people living a positive life is impossible because they have allowed the experiences of the past to shape their worldview instead of allowing the word of God to shape their perception. When we dig into God's word it should be making us more positive. We are called to be positive currents in a negative world. For most people, negative is natural. I've heard people say, "Well that's just how I am. I say it like I see it." Well, thankfully that isn't how God operates. We have to be like God and say it like He sees it! Our language should never be one of loss rather than gain. We must train our minds to believe true success is doing your best even when the odds are stacked against us and knowing God will come through! We have to understand that being positive is way more than just saying some positive faith confessions or thinking positive. It starts in our hearts. Our hearts are the ground zero for building a positive life. Jesus said it best when talking about the heart.

Luke 6:45 NLT
A good person produces good things from the treasury of a good heart, and an evil person produces evil things from the treasury of an evil heart. What you say flows from what is in your heart.

Our hearts are the treasury of our lives. Our mind processes and says what is in our hearts. So it is good to say confessions and read positive things in order to think on them, but for us to truly live positive lives we have to have positive things buried deep in our hearts. Our dreams being fulfilled is not an easy task. There will be times when you think all is lost. There will be times when people betray you and leave you with a knife hanging out of your back! There will be times when there is more month at the end of the money! Those are the times when the deep well of positivity is what you need to pull from in order to make it through! I believe the difference between people who make it and people who don't is the positivity they live out when bad things happen. You overcome negativity through practicing positivity in your words and actions. This is essential to living your dream.

• Offense is a symptom of DDS

Some people are so hurt, they can't even see the dream God has for them. They walk around as a victim rather than as a victor. They walk around with an victim mentality because of the hurt they've experienced. Well it may come as no surprise to you, but everybody has been hurt. I personally have been hurt in more ways than I'd like to remember from childhood through adulthood by people who had my trust and respect. I could easily walk in offense my entire life if I wanted to. Everyday, no matter where you go, you will have opportunities to be offended or to be forgiving. Walking in forgiveness is the antidote to offense and becoming bitter. I have known so many Christians who are just angry and bitter people because they have never let go of the offense that they still harbor maybe 5, 10, or even 20 years later! Walking in forgiveness is more than just saying we forgive someone for something. It's a lifestyle because we could be offended at every little thing.

> **WE HAVE TO BE GREAT FORGIVERS.**

If you want to know if you've forgiven someone, try this exercise. Sit back and close your eyes. Now think of someone who hurt you. What's the first thought that comes into your head. Is the thought from a place of love or hate, is it from a place of blessing or cursing? This is a true litmus test of forgiveness in our hearts. It may take may years for forgiveness to happen but the more we bless those who've hurt us, they more the healing in our hearts takes place.

Luke 6:28 NLT
Bless those who curse you. Pray for those who hurt you.

When we go through the process of our dream, we will run into people who will flat out be haters of us and of our dream. Our response to these people will be key to how we live our dream. Our motivation isn't to prove someone wrong and be fueled by offense and hatred, but it is to be motivated out of love and fueled by helping others through reaching our dream.

STOP BEING DEFICIENT

It's time we stop being deficient in our dream. If you've noticed any of these symptoms then find someone your trust and that loves you to help hold you accountable so the this deficiency doesn't override your dream. You can over come DDS by changing your mindset. It's time to renew your mind and allow yourself to dream again!

Romans 12:2 NKJV
Do not conform to the pattern of this world, but be transformed by the renewing of your mind. Then you will be able to test and approve what God's will is—his good, pleasing and perfect will.

CHAPTER 3

The Process of a Dream

Say it out loud, right now, "Trust the process." Trusting the process is one of the most grueling parts of living your dream. It breaks us down just to build us back up again. Anything that has significance has gone through a process. There is power in the process of God when we are obedient to God in our dream. The process of God is never an easy one. It really all depends on our cooperation with the Holy Spirit. We can go through different processes in life, some good and some bad. Regardless of where we are there is a process going on. The awesome thing about our dream is that we get to participate in the process and move forward with the Holy Spirit in reaching our God-given dream.

Most processes have different phases and each phase has a different purpose. The phases are there for a reason. God doesn't ever skip a phase to save us from the lesson He'd like to teach us. I can't tell you how many times in life I thought I had learned the lesson God was teaching me in an area only to find myself back in the very same place again maybe a year or two later. I sit back and think, "Well I must've failed that one!" God, in all of His mercy, love, and patience, sets the test before me once again in order that I may learn the lesson. The process is by no means to punish us! We have to get away from this punitive religious way of thinking about God. If God allows something in our lives, then it is up to us to take authority in the Spirit of God and walk through it and learn the lesson being taught. The lessons of God are always birthed out of love.

Proverbs 3:12 NLT
For the LORD corrects those he loves, just as a father corrects a child in whom he delights.

If we aren't being corrected somewhere along the way, then I'd dare to say that maybe we aren't fully walking in the love of God. I know it sounds like a harsh statement but correction from God comes from the love of God. Not punishment! Punishment isn't what God does these days. God does allow consequences but He isn't doling out punishment because of what Jesus did for us on the cross.

> **WHEN WE TRUST THE PROCESS OF GOD, WE ARE TRUSTING THE GOD OF THE PROCESS.**

The phases of a dream are prevalent all throughout scripture. We will look back on the life of Joseph and find that he had a process that may look very similar to ours. Dreams go through many different phases, from what I've experienced. but for the sake of this book I've listed six.

1. Dormant Phase

Every person has a God-given destiny inside of them. Most people live and die without ever activating that dream. They allow fear, circumstances, or other people to keep that dream dormant until one day they die and the dream never has the chance to live. You could drive through any town or major city in the world and one thing you will find is a cemetery. That cemetery holds not just the remains of those who passed, but it's a symbol of those who may or may have not lived the dream God had given them on this earth. It's a sobering picture walking up to a tombstone and see that our life is represented by a dash in between two dates.

When our time here on earth is gone we all must answer the question, "Did I fulfill God's call on my life?" God's word is clear that will receive eternal rewards based on our deeds (a much different subject than salvation, which is a free gift to all who believe and are born again). Fulfilling our call is something that we are responsible for. All of us are called to different things and maybe even called to it for different seasons as well. As a Christian, we are all given a God-given dream for our lives that only we can fulfill. Others may have similar dreams but we must realize there are over 7 billion people on the planet and only 30% are actually Christians. So if we are given a dream from God, the ultimate goal is to help people become disciples of Jesus. If your dream looks similar to or exactly like someone else's, it's ok because God needs more dreamers to reach more people!

The problem in this phase and why most people never get out of it is they settle for less. Most people get into a rut in life and just accept the norm, they accept status quo and remain dormant in their dream. Settling for less than God's best is actually unacceptable for someone who has been saved by the blood of Jesus. Here's some real talk and it may offend some of you, but hopefully it will motivate you. Settling for less than God's best is a slap in the face to what Jesus did on the cross for us! Jesus didn't die so we could JUST go to heaven. How dare we look at heaven as a benefit. It's our home! At the same time Jesus didn't die so we could eke out some small existence on this planet. He gave us the power of the Holy Spirit to live the God kind of life! That power is meant to be used to live the abundant life here on earth and to help as many people as possible to discover the love of God for themselves.

You can't reach for a dream and remain mediocre at the same time. The dream will end up stretching you

> **THE MINUTE YOU SETTLE FOR LESS THAN THE DREAM GOD GAVE YOU IS THE MINUTE YOU GET LESS THAN WHAT YOU SETTLED FOR.**

to a place where you can't be mediocre anymore. We end up settled into a routine life, living with a constant feeling of disappointment and frustration that we tend to keep at bay with temporary band-aids —junk TV, comfort food, shopping sprees, drinking, drugs, and the spiral goes downward until we are numb to God's presence and the promptings of His Holy Spirit in our lives. We look around and call what we are living "life." It's not life at all, it's an existence. Life by the biblical definition is over the top!

John 10:10 NKJV
The thief does not come except to steal, and to kill, and to destroy. I have come that they may have life, and that they may have it more abundantly.

I love this commentary from the latter part of John 10:10, "...and that they may have it more abundantly."

> "May have it more abundantly - Literally, that they may have abundance, or that which abounds. The word denotes that which is not absolutely essential to life, but which is superadded to make life happy. They shall not merely have life - simple, bare existence - but they shall have all those superadded things which are needful to make that life eminently blessed

and happy. It would be vast mercy to keep men merely from annihilation or hell; but Jesus will give them eternal joy, peace, the society of the blessed, and all those exalted means of felicity which are prepared for them in the world of glory."
-Barne's Notes on the Bible

Our call to life is abundance! Not extravagance or wastefulness but true abundance in which our lives are a blessing to others. I've seen so many people start moving forward out of this phase and immediately get hit with disappointment so they give up almost instantly. Frustration sets in and they just keep living the same existence, calling it "life." Disappointment is the gap that exists between expectation and reality. Frustration is when your expectation and your experience are polarized. At some point along the way we must break free from disappointment, frustration, and whatever else is holding us back and just keep at our dream. Everyone has a dream and when people get to the place where they get tired of "life" as normal they move to this next phase.

2. Discovery Phase

No matter where you are in life you can live your dream. In my short life, I've found that the most fruitful dreams, the dreams that have changed the world for God's kingdom always started with a dream from God. Wow, deep right? The thing is... I can't tell you how many people come with some cooky concoction of a dream and they try to convince everybody else around them it's from God! There is both a vast difference and a fine line between fantasy and a God-given dream. Sometimes we may have eaten a bad piece of pizza and wake up with some cooky "dream." Fantasy is something that we have dreamed up and isn't something could possibly happen. A God-given dream is something that will fit into the unique gifting and talent that God has given you in order for you to help people get connected to Him. A God-given dream will be birthed out of a healthy relationship with God. When we are spending time in God's presence we will discover His dream for us.

> **GOD'S DREAM FOR US WILL COME THROUGH THE PROCESS OF DISCOVERING WHO WE ARE IN CHRIST.**

We discover who we are by figuring what we do well and what we do terribly. I can't speak for anyone else but hopefully you can learn a little from my own experience in the discovery phase. When I first discovered God's dream and call for my life, I was completely lost. I was a high school dropout, completely addicted to drugs, and trying to find love in all the wrong places. When I saw my youth pastor preaching his heart and heard that still small voice say to my heart, "You're going to do that," it wasn't a real burning bush experience or anything. I just knew in my heart that I was supposed to be a communicator for God. At the time, I was about as introverted as you could get. I didn't like people at all, I had never been up in front of a group of people as a public speaker, and truly didn't know the first thing about ministry or God for that matter! So what did I do from there?

I endeavored to learn as much as possible. I started serving and expressed to my youth pastor what I had experienced. He then helped set me on a journey to fulfill that call. A true leader will help you fulfill your dreams, not just have you fulfill theirs. I was given opportunities to serve and lead in my local church. Eventually I was given more opportunities with more responsibility such as leading worship and speaking. Eventually, as I matured in walking with God and matured in the gift of communication, God started using me tremendously. I was living part of God's dream for my life.

My life has had a few layers and many different twists and turns to the dream God gave me. As with most dreams, there will be pieces and parts that you won't understand until you have lived through it and are able to look at it in hindsight.

> **VERY RARELY DOES A DREAM GO FROM POINT A TO POINT B, IT TYPICALLY STOPS AT EVERY LETTER IN THE ALPHABET!**

I know I mentioned this earlier but after serving as a youth pastor for a number of years, God placed me in a position that I had never been in before: graphic designer. I couldn't understand it, but I've always had a knack for what looks cool. When I designed that flyer for the youth event, and then said "Yes" to designing my pastor's next sermon series DVD cover, God opened a whole new level to living my dream. I became more talented as a designer, then it flowed into web design, then it flowed into marketing, then it flowed into video editing, and eventually it birthed a design company I still own and operate to this very day! When we say, "Yes" to God He then will open opportunities to us that we never could have imagined!

Through all this I've found that God was preparing me to lead my own church and company. With it would come books, websites, speaking engagements, training events, and the list goes on. But all of it was birthed out of discovering what I did well and staying away from what I did terribly. I'm not against further education but I've found that with or without schooling you can accomplish your dream! Get as much education in your field as possible, but success will truly come from God's training for reigning! I'm still pushing to grow and learn. I'm looking towards a generational legacy. I believe that God's dream on our lives is bigger than a lifetime on earth will permit!

3. Delayed Phase

After the exciting phase of discovery we find ourselves at the next phase in the process. Say it out loud one more time for me, "Trust the process." I want you to get that phrase deep down in your spirit because when we get into this phase, we'll be relying on God more than ever.

So here we are. God has spoken to us and we are off to the races! Or so we think. Throughout the process of the dream, delay is inevitable. God is a good Father and He is always trying to disciple us and teach us if we are open to it. He will use anything to do it.

> **THROUGH THE DELAYS OF GOD WE CAN SEE THE LOVE OF GOD.**

Divine delays are a part of God's plan. Even in our everyday life, divine delays can save us from tragedy! I've always wondered why some people excel in life so quick and others don't. I may not know the full answer but I think part of it has to do with the lessons we learn along the way. These are the divine delays God is wanting us to take note of in the journey of living the dream.

I can just imagine Joseph's excitement and anticipation of the dream God had given him. He probably started acting like the ruler of a nation right then and there! He may have been telling all the sheep to bow down, the rocks and sage brushes to bow down. He was amped up that his brothers would have to bow down too! His arrogance is probably what got him to the point of having his brothers hate him so much. Let's jump back to our biblical narrative and find out where Joseph is in the process of his dream.

Genesis 37:18-23 NKJV
Now when they saw him afar off, even before he came near them, they conspired against him to kill him. Then they said to one another, "Look, this dreamer is coming! Come therefore, let us now kill him and cast him into some pit; and we shall say, 'Some wild beast has devoured him.' We shall see what will become of his dreams!" But Reuben heard it, and he delivered him out of their hands, and said, "Let us not kill him." And Reuben said to them, "Shed no blood, but cast him into this pit which is in the wilderness, and do not lay a hand on him"—that he might deliver him out of their hands, and bring him back to his father. So it came to pass, when Joseph had come to his brothers, that they stripped Joseph of his tunic, the tunic of many colors that was on him. Then they took him and cast him into a pit. And the pit was empty; there was no water in it.

Joseph has this amazing dream and his dad gives him this awesome coat – life is good. So let's live the dream! Well, not so fast. Here's where God's dream for Joseph takes its first major delay. His brothers hate him and decide they've had quite enough of Joseph and his dream. They throw him in a pit and leave him for dead!

No dream fulfilled yet.

Let's find out what happens next…

Genesis 37:25-28 NKJV
And they sat down to eat a meal. Then they lifted their eyes and looked, and there was a company of Ishmaelites, coming from Gilead with their camels, bearing spices, balm, and myrrh, on their way to carry them down to Egypt. So Judah said to his brothers, "What profit is there if we kill our brother and conceal his blood? Come and let us sell him to the Ishmaelites, and let not our hand be upon him, for he is our brother and our flesh." And his brothers listened. Then Midianite traders passed by; so the brothers pulled Joseph up and lifted him out of the pit, and sold him to the Ishmaelites for twenty shekels of silver. And they took Joseph to Egypt.

So now we see that Joseph's brothers had so much contempt for him that they were sitting down and eating, actually enjoying a meal together while their brother was in the pit they had just thrown him into and were going to leave him for dead! It makes me wonder if there was a really awkward silence while they were all sitting there. Like, we all know what's going on but let's overlook the big fat white elephant in the room. That's what happens when we have a dream in our life and it isn't being fulfilled. It's a big white elephant of a dream!

Anyway, back to the story – Joseph gets thrown into the pit, but instead of just being done with him, his brothers decide they may as well profit off of their brother's disappearance. So not only did these guys hate their brother so much that they wanted to get rid of him, they actually made money from their dirty deeds! This is probably about as far away from Joseph's original dream as you can get. No dream fulfilled yet. Let's keep moving forward and see what happens next.

4. Derailed Phase

Genesis 39:19-20 NKJV
So it was, when his master heard the words which his wife spoke to him, saying, "Your servant did to me after this manner," that his anger was aroused. Then Joseph's master took him and put him into the prison, a place where the king's prisoners were confined. And he was there in the prison.

So here we find the tail end of a story that I write more about in detail in chapter five. The short story is that Joseph has been accused of raping Potiphar's wife. The backstory is that the Midianites sold Joseph as a slave to one of Egypt's high commanding officer's named Potiphar. Joseph oversaw everything in Potiphar's house, including tending to his wife's needs. Well as the process of dream preparation would have it, Potiphar's wife had Joseph wrongly accused and thrown in jail! So again this is not moving in the direction of the dream Joseph had seen years earlier.

No dream yet. It seems like it's getting worse for Joseph! Derailment is can only happen two ways, either self-inflicted or others-inflicted.

Regardless of how it happens, when the dream goes off the rails, it seems like everything you've worked for is at a complete standstill. In my case I've had moments in my life where derailment has been self-inflicted through some really bad choices. I can blame it on my parents, people from my past, or any other emotional wound that would make sense, but ultimately taking personal responsibility for our choices is what gets us to the most healthy and honest place in life.

In Joseph's case, he was derailed by someone else. Someone else had taken control of a certain season in Joseph's life and seemingly derailed his destiny. The awesome thing about a dream is that every season is considered preparation to God. Potiphar's wife may have been able to control a small portion of Joseph's life, but she was unable to control his destiny. When our life is in God's control, there is no person that can keep us from God's will.

I remember when I was working for one of the largest churches in the nation. I was on the creative team and was doing some great work as a designer and a leader. As large staff transitions go, our lead pastors brought in another person to oversee the team I was on and helping lead. At first we seemed to have a friendly relationship but eventually things turned sour pretty quick. Before long, we were butting heads pretty regularly. So here I am working for this newly assigned authority who just seems to shoot down my designs, my ideas, piles up more work, and really made my life pretty rough. I'll admit I wasn't the best employee at that time. I had a bad attitude and my productivity sank, along with my passion and creativity. Time and time again we would try to work through it which I had hoped solved the problem. Unfortunately it didn't. I start hearing things about me that just weren't true.

Some of those things landed me in hot water and put my position on staff in some major jeopardy. I wanted to be a peacemaker. I asked to move to another area of ministry where the other gifts on my life could flourish and help further the cause of the church. That idea was met with opposition as well. I was frustrated. I was in what many would consider a dream job. I was designing for a living, making a difference in the lives of people and making great money. it seemed things were going so well until this one person came along. I started blaming this one individual for all the drama in my life and really had some nasty things in my heart towards them. I learned a lot from that experience. I learned about motives and perception. How people perceive you is how they receive you. The people in that environment saw me a certain way because of past behavior or a certain negative reaction I displayed and unfortunately most people will never be able to see past that and that's ok!

> **YOUR DESTINY ISN'T DEPENDENT UPON SOMEONE ELSE'S PERCEPTION OF YOU.**

Listen, when you start blaming just one person for the derailment of your dream then you are sorely missing the point, you are missing the preparation process of God. There is no one that can stop God's plan for you! At this juncture, I didn't take into consideration the season I was in. This was the derailment part of the dream. This was when everything that was going right goes wrong. It was part of God's process for my life. Eventually, I knew my time there was coming to a close. I knew the Holy Spirit was moving me out and I was fearful for the future. It was a mutual parting of ways and but

I was without a job and a church home. It was a feeling of complete abandonment and betrayal. I struggled for several weeks feeling like God had forgotten about me but little did I know He was working things out in the background. After a while, I had to learn how to rest in His sovereignty. Then one day, God moved. He connected me to one person who eventually connected me to another and from there it was like God launched me to the next level of my destiny and dream! I won't go into the specifics but it was God who worked everything out and I was seeing His faithfulness left and right! I could have blamed that guy over and over, but instead I trusted the process of God. I learned that I couldn't blame an entire church for my bad experience. I love the leadership, they are wonderful people who played a great part in my life and we are friendly to this day. I've learned when something seemingly bad happens to us, we must remember to embrace the process!

5. Dead Phase

Unfortunately this next phase is one that most, if not all, successful people have experienced. This is when we experience complete and total loss and devastation. What happens when everything you've worked for goes up in flames? What happens when all the people you thought you could trust turn their back on you and walk out? What happens when all the money and possessions you have in the whole wide world get taken from you? What do you do when the dream seemingly dies?

This is what happened to Joseph, and honestly what happened to me. Joseph had a dream and that dream cost him everything he knew. His brothers betrayed him and threw him into a pit. His master's wife lied on him and threw him into prison. At what point do you give up on the dream? At what point do you think maybe it's time to stop dreaming? Never.

Similarly for me, I went through a horrific season when I thought my dream was dead. It was a self-inflicted derailment that got me there, but when it rains it surely pours. Everything I had worked for went up in flames. The church I had planted closed down. The network I had built over twenty years was severely damaged. The finances I had accumulated were gone. Even the possessions I had were carried out of my house by other people! And worst of all my marriage was over and my family was gone. I walked into an empty shell of a home and I was devastated. The dream was dead…or at least, that's what I thought.

I have found that dreams don't die, they only await to be lived. There are seasons in which we think the dream is dead. God is done with us, we are finished. I might as well go back to living the life I was before I found Him, because it doesn't seem like He's listening anymore. I wrote this book to tell you, sir or ma'am, if you have a breath in your lungs and a beat in your heart, your dream is alive and kicking! Just because we go through seasons where things seem dead does not mean they are. You will make it through the dead season.

6. Divine Phase

After experiencing total loss and devastation, I fell asleep that night and though it was restless, I still woke up the next morning. You know what I found out? The sun was still shining, the birds were still chirping away, the cars were still bustling along. Life had not stopped just because everything in my world fell apart. To me, this was a sign that everything was going to be ok. I had to move forward, because I didn't have any other viable options.

I can only imagine the devastation the disciples felt on the first two days after Jesus was crucified and left for dead on the cross and buried in a borrowed tomb. It must have been the darkest season of their lives at this point. This was the Messiah, the one who was to redeem this broken world, but instead he's dead and buried. Like our dream, He's in the tomb so we might as well start the mourning process.

Before that first tear sheds from our eye, God already knows the beginning and the end. He already knows what is going to happen. God has an interesting way of working. It's as if we get to the point of complete exhaustion, complete abandonment, complete loss, when everything seems completely destroyed – and that's when He steps in.

1 Corinthians 1:26-31 NKJV
For you see your calling, brethren, that not many wise according to the flesh, not many mighty, not many noble, are called. But God has chosen the foolish things of the world to put to shame the wise, and God has chosen the weak things of the world to put to shame the things which are mighty; and the base things of the world and the things which are despised God has chosen, and the things which are not, to bring to nothing the things that are, that no flesh should glory in His presence. But of Him you are in Christ Jesus, who became for us wisdom from God—and righteousness and sanctification and redemption— that, as it is written, "He who glories, let him glory in the Lord."

God uses devastating situations to bring us back to a place of glory so that only He can get the credit. I want people to look at my life and say, "Only God could have done that." There's no greater thing that could happen, no world-renowned award, no amount of money, no global network, nothing that could ever take the place of a life that has been fully restored, redeemed, and resurrected, and God gets all the glory for it.

> **WHEN SOMEONE LOOKS AT YOUR LIFE AND THEY SAY, "ONLY GOD", THEN YOU KNOW YOU'RE ON THE RIGHT TRACK.**

When Jesus walked the earth he raised people from the dead. People are dreams. My family is a dream to me, my children are a dream to me, my church is a dream to me. Helping them reach their destiny is my dream. When Jesus raised people from the dead he was bringing dreams and destinies back to life.

Matthew 9:23-25 NIV
When Jesus entered the synagogue leader's house and saw the noisy crowd and people playing pipes, he said, "Go away. The girl is not dead but asleep." But they laughed at him. After the crowd had been put outside, he went in and took the girl by the hand, and she got up.

The context of this story is absolutely heartbreaking. This is basically a little girl's pre-funeral. The girl had died and people had started the mourning process. In the Hebrew culture the playing of a dirge just after someone had died was commonplace. The next step was a funeral. This was when Jesus showed up at this leader's house and began the process of raising the dead. Notice there were three things that Jesus did.

1. He cleared the atmosphere.

When Jesus entered the synagogue leader's house and saw the noisy crowd and people playing pipes, he said, "Go away."

Jesus cleared the atmosphere of death. He got rid of people that were playing the mourning songs because he didn't even want a hint of death hanging around. The only thing on His mind was life! It's time that we have a life-giving mentality about our future! When we enter the next season of divinity for our life, we need to clear out every dead thing that would try and remind us of our past. This will include losing some "friends," getting rid of some folks on social media, clearing out some old pictures, writing an email or a card in order to bring closure. Whatever you have to do to clear the atmosphere in your life, do it. We can't experience the divine process of God while we still have the lingering scent of death in the air.

2. He spoke words of faith.

"The girl is not dead but asleep." But they laughed at him.

Jesus spoke exactly what he believed. The bible tells us in Matthew 12:34 that *"for out of the abundance of the heart the mouth speaks."* Jesus said what was in his heart. It is so important that we believe the words of faith that we speak. We must get to the point in our journey with God that when we speak a promise, regardless of whether we see it happening or not, that we truly believe it!

The next part is that they laughed at him. Can you imagine laughing at Jesus? Laughing at the Savior and Creator of the world? Talk about short-sightedness. These people couldn't see what was right in front of them! When you start speaking words of faith, people will laugh at you. They will call you naïve. They will make you think that you are crazy and are making a bad decision. When God gives you a promise, you need to believe it and then speak it. Don't ever allow anyone to say anything contradictory to what God has told you.

3. He produced the miraculous.

After the crowd had been put outside, he went in and took the girl by the hand, and she got up.

Jesus did exactly what he said he would do. When everything is stripped away and you think the dream is dead, it's done, and it's just not gonna happen...Jesus steps in. Jesus walks into the picture grabs you by the hand and helps you get up.

Jacob thought his son was Joseph was dead, but he wasn't. The people thought Lazarus was dead but he wasn't. The roman soldier thought his little girl was dead but she wasn't. The synagogue leader thought his daughter was dead, but she wasn't. Sometimes it takes the death season to awaken us to what we were truly created for. Then Jesus steps in and brings it back to life.

God will breathe new life into a situation and give you a budding hope for the future. God will not forget about you. He will provide a beacon of light and hope in the darkest of storms and no matter what anybody else says, it does not matter. I've found that words are cheap, but love truly does something. God will bring you that new relationship. God will raise to life that dream of a ministry or business. The same God who raised Jesus from the dead is the same God who will raise us up and bring us to a divine place of living the dream he has called us to!

You might be in a dead season right now, but I want you to know that tomorrow the sun will still shine and the birds will still sing. Time will keep moving forward and you must do the same. He is more than the God of restoration or renewal, He is the God of resurrection and He will bring dead things back to life!

CHAPTER 4

Breaking the Dreamer

What happens when God actually answers your prayer? What happens when God actually gives you the blessing of a new job, new position, or new spouse? It's interesting because the blessing is also the breaking. The blessing will require more of us than we would've ever imagined.

One thing I find interesting as a father is that my kids never leave a gift unopened at Christmas time. As a matter of fact, I have to pull the reins back just to keep them from opening their gifts too early. They complain and whine about it, but I know that there's a time and a place for their gift to be unwrapped. Before the appointed hour, it's not the right time and it's not the right environment. I believe that God does the same thing with us. He has given us the gift of a dream, a talent, an ability, something that we want to tear into and show everybody around us what we've received – but more often than not, it's too early. It's not the right time and it's not the right environment.

A number of years ago I experienced a season of restoration after a major breakdown. I was ready to get back into ministry in a full-time capacity. I was anxious to jump in and preach, pastor, lead and go full steam ahead with the call of God on my life. The problem was, the leadership that God had placed in my life didn't think so. Not only did they not think so, the opportunities for me to even attempt that sort of ministry were few are far between with no mentoring or discipleship involved. All around me were people that (in my arrogant and extremely prideful estimation) were less talented, less influential, didn't know near as much about leadership that I did, but yet they were doing the thing I so desperately wanted to do. I was so frustrated, I whined and complained to God and even those around me who I thought could help me get this gift opened a little early – but it wasn't the right time and it wasn't the right environment. When my kids tried to open a gift too early there were always consequences for disobedience. The same thing happens to us, and the same thing happened to Joseph.

Genesis 40:14-15 NIV
But when all goes well with you, remember me and show me kindness; mention me to Pharaoh and get me out of this prison. I was forcibly carried off from the land of the Hebrews, and even here I have done nothing to deserve being put in a dungeon.

Genesis 40:23 NIV
The chief cupbearer, however, did not remember Joseph; he forgot him.

Here we find Joseph in prison for about 5-10 years for a crime he didn't commit. He sees these two cellmates who looked very troubled, so he asks them what's wrong. He learns that these two men each had dreams. One dream was awesome and the other was awful. Joseph wanted to help these guys out, so he asks them to tell him their dreams. It's interesting that in verse 14 Joseph barters a deal with the guy BEFORE he interprets the dream. Joseph is pleading his case with a guy who can't do anything about his situation. How many times do we complain to someone about something they can't fix for us? Before long we start to wallow in gossip and bitterness.

Joseph was basically selling the gift on his life in order to profit from it, instead of giving it away freely. I wonder if it would have turned out different if Joseph had interpreted the dream, and *then* asked the guy to remember mentioning him to Pharaoh. It was a test of the heart for Joseph here. Joseph was desperate to get out of his current circumstance so he started wheeling and dealing with whomever he thought could get him out of his current predicament. I can't blame him. I've been there before. I have been so dejected and desperate that I have done the same thing. Every time I tried though, God would shut it down. I'd apply for this job at a huge design firm or try and make something happen with this client or that church. God would always shut it down.

Every. Single. Time.

The same thing happened to Joseph. It's as if Joseph was losing faith that things would work out. So he was looking to the butler imprisoned with him to get him out of there instead of God. Think about that, he was trying to make a deal with a guy who was in the same predicament. The butler gets released, but Joseph sits in prison for another two years. Think about this. Joseph changed this guy's life! He told him his whole life was about to be restored and it was. Don't you think this guy thought about Joseph all the time? I would. But for "some convenient reason" he forgot about Joseph instead. I'd say God intervened in order to show Joseph that this was His plan and not Joseph's. When we say we are committed to God and we are all sold out on His plan for our life, then we should expect Him to intervene at times when we think He shouldn't. God will make sure that the stage is set and the audience is ready in order for you to operate in your gift. God will prepare your platform.

> **BEFORE GOD PREPARES OUR PLATFORM HE PREPARES US.**

MY ACHY BREAKY HEART

Psalm 51:17 NIV
My sacrifice, O God, is a broken spirit;
a broken and contrite heart
you, God, will not despise.

Living your dream usually starts with refining the dreamer. God is into preparation. He prepares us for our dream long before the dream takes place. When you truly have a God-given dream it will come with a process of refinement. God uses different phases, seasons, and processes to allow His dream for us to come forth… but He always starts with the heart. Usually our heart has to be broken before any significant work can take place. I know that makes no sense at the moment but it will soon. Keep reading.

A broken heart can be the matrix of greatness, if we respond correctly. A broken heart can happen a number of different ways, whether through a crushed dream, a destroyed relationship, or a devastating circumstance. Of course having our hearts broken is painful and no one wants to go through the process. It's the same paradox of wanting to go to heaven but not wanting to die. We all want the benefits of greatness but not all of us are willing to go through the process of getting there. If we are to achieve our dream and truly live our God-given destiny then there will be one or more seasons of brokenness that we will need to go through. That's right, we probably won't have our heart broken just once, but multiple times. Again this is the seed of greatness. There is something miraculous and supernatural that happens when a broken heart is handed to a loving God. It's like God takes all of those little shattered and broken pieces of our hearts and buries them as seed for our future.

Matthew 21:44 NIV
"Anyone who falls on this stone will be broken to pieces; anyone on whom it falls will be crushed."

In context, this verse is speaking to those who have accepted or rejected Jesus and the message of the gospel, but in our context of the process of a dream it works as well. The first part of this verse has a very passive beginning. It implies that a stone is laying there with no movement or momentum. Therefore it affords the opportunity to be used as a hard surface for an something to be thrown upon and broken. The latter part of the verse implies movement of the stone heading towards an intended target. Guess where the bullseye is? That's right. You. Brokenness can come from any direction, but it's up to us to choose it. Brokenness is a choice that can birth greatness when we embrace it..

When you choose brokenness, you voluntarily throw yourself on Jesus so He can break down your pride and sin for the sole purpose of building you back up in His likeness. Being crushed? Well not so much. That comes out of nowhere and catches you out of the blue! The sooner you realize you have been crushed and accept the humbling process, the sooner you can get up and move forward. One is voluntary and the other is not. Both are extremely painful, but both can produce the same results if we are willing to walk through the process.

As I was doing research on the process of brokenness, I came across an interesting article on how people break horses in order to ride them. It noted that a horse is ready to begin the process once it turns two years old. From this point on through the breaking experience, the young horse is exposed to new sights, sounds, feelings and expectations. This time is crucial because it decides whether a horse will be an excellent or poor mount. Likewise with us, the process of being broken is up to us. We get to determine how long or short the process is, and we get to determine how hard or easy it is as well. It all depends on how we respond to the breaking. Our habits will determine our attitudes.

> **BROKENNESS CAN PRODUCE BITTERNESS OR GREATNESS. IT CAN KEEP US FROM OUR DREAM OR PROPEL US TOWARD OUR DREAM.**

We were created for freedom, to live a limitless life. Even in the Garden of Eden, when God created Adam and Eve, He created them naked. We were created to be unencumbered and without limits. I'm a fan of clothes – I'm not saying we should all join nudist colonies. Uh, no thanks! But what I am saying is that the original design for us is to be free from limits and limitations. Unfortunately we are born into a world where freedom resembles rebellion. Being born into a sinful world produces in us sinful attitudes and behaviors by default. That's why when we are "born again" there is a progressive process of grace that we get to take part in by renewing our minds according to God's word. As we start to dream and get motivated to move forward with that dream, God steps in and basically says, "You get to move forward with that dream but that bad attitude isn't going with you, that unforgiveness isn't going with you and that pride certainly isn't going with you."

There are all types of things that can't move with us as we move into living our dream. This is because God wants us to move in purity. Purity of heart, mind, soul, and motive.

God shut Joseph down because his motive wasn't pure. At some point along the way, that extra two years he was in prison, Joseph must have gotten his heart right. Our hearts being right may not look like we think. We think it's this shiny, all white, completely pure thing, but maybe in fact, it's beat up, broken, and bruised so God can actually put it back together again. Maybe being broken isn't the goal but it is sure part of the process. Being refined is allowing God to truly purify us.

WHAT ARE YOU SEEKING?

As mentioned earlier, we have to get the sobering answer to the question, "Is our dream only about us?" If the answer is "yes," then we have a long road of refinement and brokenness ahead of us. If the answer is "no," then our motives will be tested on that answer. Either way God will make sure our motives are pure concerning the dream He has given us. Remember we are given His dream for our lives.

Jeremiah 17:9 NKJV
"The heart is deceitful above all things,
And desperately wicked;
Who can know it?

This scripture is relevant to this conversation because God is the one who knows our hearts. He is the only one sometimes – not even ourselves. Our hearts can be so deceitful. This is why we lie and don't follow through sometimes. Our intentions are good and we want to follow through, but the motive resides in our hearts and we live our lives out of our hearts. So we must destroy or, more politely, de-construct the dream. We need to weed out anything that even has a scent of selfish flesh on it. Our dream should be all Holy

Spirit, it should be all God. Whatever is in there that has the possibility of getting our fingerprints all over God's glory must go. Typically when dreams seem to have been destroyed or de-constructed right before our very eyes it is because they have become idols in our life. We often end up worshipping the dream instead of the Giver of the dream. The dream itself becomes the focus instead of God.

Matthew 6:33 NKJV
But seek first the kingdom of God and His righteousness, and all these things shall be added to you.

It's all a matter of what or, more appropriately, WHO we are seeking. Our focus is key at this point. We need to be focused on God and His plan for us. This doesn't mean to become legalistically religious but it means to truly have God in our thoughts so that the life we live is a praise and a worship unto Him! We need to be thinking on God all the time. Out of this thinking will come ideas, plans, and strategies for the dream he has given us. We must temper our drive and passion with the fruit of the Spirit in order for God to do the heavy lifting when it comes to our dream. Some people get so burned out because they think it's up to them to make a God-given dream come to pass.

> **IT'S UP TO GOD TO MAKE THE DREAM COME TO PASS. IT'S UP TO US TO BE OBEDIENT THROUGH THE PROCESS.**

Let's backtrack a bit here in Joseph's story. This passage of scripture was just before Joseph was thrown into a pit and left for dead by his brothers. It was also after Joseph had the dream God had given him.

Genesis 37:14-17 NKJV
Then he said to him, "Please go and see if it is well with your brothers and well with the flocks, and bring back word to me." So he sent him out of the Valley of Hebron, and he went to Shechem. Now a certain man found him, and there he was, wandering in the field. And the man asked him, saying, "What are you seeking?" So he said, "I am seeking my brothers. Please tell me where they are feeding their flocks." And the man said, "They have departed from here, for I heard them say, 'Let us go to Dothan.'" So Joseph went after his brothers and found them in Dothan.

I love this passage; this whole story would have made sense if it wasn't in there but it's in there on purpose. Joseph's father sent him on a mission, just as our heavenly Father sends us out on a mission. Joseph's father gave him specific instructions as to where to go and what to do. God usually does the same thing with us from time to time concerning direction for our lives. Notice the scripture says he was "wandering in the field." Joseph was wandering, just kind of out there like most ADHD dreamers in the kingdom. Out there wandering around like, "Oh, look at the clouds and the birds, and... a squirrel!" How familiar does this sound? We are given specific instructions either through the Bible or even a *rhema* (God-spoken) word in our lives with specific directions, and yet we end up wandering. We wander in our purpose, we wander in our finances, we wander in our marriage, we wander in our minds and our hearts. All this wandering is unproductive and even destructive to our dream! Wandering seems passive but it is in fact a strategy of the enemy to keep us distracted from our primary purpose!

Again this whole story of Joseph and the betrayal of his brothers would have made perfect sense without this interaction. But watch what happens in the scripture. It says, "Now a certain man found him, and there he was, wandering in the field. And the man asked him, saying, "What are you seeking?"

When we have a dream, we will run into all kinds of people. We will run into spiritually weird people who have visions of Jesus riding unicorns, we will have doubters of us and haters of our dreams, but once in a great while we will have people we don't really even know come into our lives and say one phrase that gets our trajectory back on course and changes our lives for the good. That's what happened to Joseph. Joseph ran into this guy and the one question set him back on course, "What are you seeking?" Sometimes it takes someone to come into our lives and ask, "What are you seeking?" The answer to this question is vital. The answer is a test to see if we are operating in obedience and it answers our ultimate motive. It gets us back on track, it gets us focused on the task at hand. Motives are a major key to living your God-given dream. So, Joseph followed the man's directions and found his brothers in Dothan and we know what happens at this point!

Genesis 37:18-20 NKJV
Now when they saw him afar off, even before he came near them, they conspired against him to kill him. Then they said to one another, "Look, this dreamer is coming! Come therefore, let us now kill him and cast him into some pit; and we shall say, 'Some wild beast has devoured him.' We shall see what will become of his dreams!"

His brothers spot him in the distance and come up with a plan to destroy Joseph and his dream! So much for following that guy's advice! I can't tell you how many times someone has given me advice and I follow it and the short-term outcome is negative. I want to kick myself and think, "I'm never going to listen to that person again!" It makes me wonder if Joseph thought the same thing. "I was fine wandering out there in the field! Why did I listen to that guy!? Now here I am in a pit left for dead! I should've never listened to him." I've felt that way before and I bet you have too. This is important because the mistakes we make or the unfortunate turn of events we find ourselves in are all a part of our story. Joseph needed to listen to this guy because it was destined for him to be betrayed in order for his dream to come to pass.

This is where the rubber meets the road. We have to take into account everything that happens to us as seed for our future. We can't fall into blaming people around us or blaming life in general. "Well if I was born into a different family, I wouldn't be this way. Well if I wasn't taken advantage of as a kid, I wouldn't have this addiction." And the list goes on. I'm not trying to be insensitive to your circumstance. Believe me, I've needed mercy in my own circumstance before. We must understand that our circumstances don't determine our destiny – they only prepare us for it. God has a huge destiny for you. He has something magnificent prepared, but we must trust in our all-loving Father. We must believe that what we are going through and experiencing, are all contributing to the greater glory which will reveal our story! There is no testimony without the test! There is no glory without the story!

Let me reiterate that everybody wants greatness, but most are unwilling to go through what it takes to achieve it. If you find yourself in one or more seasons of brokenness then rejoice!

This means that God is adding content to your story. One chapter of a book doesn't tell the whole story! It's just a chapter. He is weaving these trials and tribulations into the fabric of your life as part of the greatness He is building in you! Our lives are like a tapestry of grace. The front may look amazing but if you turn it around you'll see threads going all sorts of directions with no pattern at all!

Don't quit now. Keep pushing through every hard time. God has destined you to win! Your story is far from over. He is still weaving your tapestry and when He is done, all will see the masterpiece of the Lord on your life!

CHAPTER 5

Dream Roadblocks

Living your dream is not going to be easy, but it is worth it. Our heart is usually our biggest hindrance to living our dream. I've found that we all encounter various roadblocks that can keep us from living our dream. My list may look different from yours, but I think all of us can identify with at least a few. Living your dream or having a successful life is what God wants for all of us. I define success as doing better than I was before, in my heart, my mind, and my world around me. Notice I didn't say if I was richer, more famous, or any of the exterior trappings of success. We can go through the worst seasons of our lives successfully because if our hearts are healthy, then our souls will be healthy as well! The interesting thing is that when our hearts are doing well everything else on our outside will eventually begin doing well too. It's a matter of perspective. Keeping our joy level high. Keeping our words positive. Keeping our motives pure. These are what help you stay on the roadmap for success and get through your roadblocks to success. True success is when God elevates you. When our hearts are right then God will do the elevating because when our time comes, He knows we will be ready.

Not by any means is this list exhaustive but I've listed sixteen roadblocks to people living their dreams and the solutions to each one. So let's jump right in!

1. The Roadblock of Betrayal & Bitterness - The Solution is Forgiveness

Genesis 39:6-23 NKJV
Thus he left all that he had in Joseph's hand, and he did not know what he had except for the bread which he ate. Now Joseph was handsome in form and appearance. And it came to pass after these things that his master's wife cast longing eyes on Joseph, and she said, "Lie with me." But he

refused and said to his master's wife, "Look, my master does not know what is with me in the house, and he has committed all that he has to my hand. There is no one greater in this house than I, nor has he kept back anything from me but you, because you are his wife. How then can I do this great wickedness, and sin against God?" So it was, as she spoke to Joseph day by day, that he did not heed her, to lie with her or to be with her. But it happened about this time, when Joseph went into the house to do his work, and none of the men of the house was inside, that she caught him by his garment, saying, "Lie with me." But he left his garment in her hand, and fled and ran outside. And so it was, when she saw that he had left his garment in her hand and fled outside, that she called to the men of her house and spoke to them, saying, "See, he has brought in to us a Hebrew to mock us. He came in to me to lie with me, and I cried out with a loud voice. And it happened, when he heard that I lifted my voice and cried out, that he left his garment with me, and fled and went outside." So she kept his garment with her until his master came home. Then she spoke to him with words like these, saying, "The Hebrew servant whom you brought to us came in to me to mock me; so it happened, as I lifted my voice and cried out, that he left his garment with me and fled outside." So it was, when his master heard the words which his wife spoke to him, saying, "Your servant did to me after this manner," that his anger was aroused. Then Joseph's master took him and put him into the prison, a place where the king's prisoners were confined. And he was there in the prison. But the Lord was with Joseph and showed him mercy, and He gave him favor in the sight of the keeper of the prison. And the keeper of the prison committed to Joseph's hand all the prisoners who were in the prison; whatever they did there, it was his doing. The keeper of the prison did not look into anything that was under Joseph's authority, because the Lord was with him; and whatever he did, the Lord made it prosper.

So here's Joseph with his TV debut on "The Real Desperate Housewives of Egypt." Just for fun, let's just call Potiphar's wife "Hotiphar." So this cougar Hotiphar is bored or lonely or whatever and decides that Joseph is what she wants. Being a woman who gets what she wants, she finally decides it's time for her to get Joseph. Joseph being a man of God and integrity resists her day after day. He is a young man and we should give him major props for resisting! I'm sure he was fearful of the consequences if he did consent to the sexual advances of Hotiphar, but more than that, he truly wanted to please God. Joseph is doing the right thing. He was an honorable man and he was honoring those who were in authority over him. He's not doing anything wrong! He gets thrown into prison for doing the right thing. There are tens of thousands of men and women in prison who claim innocence but this guy truly was not guilty. He felt the sting of betrayal for doing the right thing. I've found betrayal is a part of seeing your dream come true.

> **THERE WILL BE PEOPLE THAT COME INTO YOUR LIFE FOR THE SOLE PURPOSE OF BETRAYING YOU.**

They don't even know it. Most of the time the betrayer doesn't even think they've done anything wrong. Every person who's done something great for God has had a betrayer. Like T.D. Jakes says, "That Judas will be close enough... to kiss you, baby." Jesus had Judas and we aren't above our Master. So we have a choice. Get bitter or get better. Betrayal is a primary source of bitterness in the lives of people. Most bitter and unhappy people you meet are that way because they were betrayed somewhere along the journey of life and never got to the solution and overcame it.

How do you get past betrayal and bitterness? The first step is to stop waiting on an apology, because it is never gonna happen! It's very rare that someone has the humility to apologize for an act of betrayal. The next step is to pray for them. Jesus said that we are to bless those who curse us. Trust me, this is hard to actually pray blessing over someone you'd much rather see destroyed, but this is what our Savior (the Savior who died for no just cause, but for our sins) has instructed us to do. As we do this we start to find forgiveness blooming in our hearts. This may be a daily thing we must practice for years in order to see a great harvest of forgiveness, but it is worth it. How do you know if you've forgiven someone? The answer to that lies in the first thought that pops in your head when you hear their name or see their picture. This is a good indicator on how far we've come in the process of forgiveness.

2. The Roadblock of Lacking Character - The Solution is Integrity

Most people in Joseph's position would have caved. A rich, influential woman coming on to you. A woman who can make all your selfish ambitions come true. A position that could put you further up the food chain. All you have to do is trade your integrity and indulge in a moment of sexual fulfillment. Many men greater than me have fallen into that. It's easy to sit back and make a judgment about those who have traded their integrity for selfishness, but until you've been in that position it's impossible to know what any of us would do. We just don't know how strong our character really is until it is tested.

The key to overcoming this roadblock is having integrity. Having integrity means having strong character. It's similar to building something with wood. The integrity of the structure is based on the strength of the wood. The integrity of our life is based on the strength of our character. We strengthen our character by spending time with God, reading His word, and being placed in situations that require strong character. Developing integrity comes through doing one right thing at a time, over and over again. As we continue to build our character God knows when we can handle the blessing of the dream. Our character is what will sustain us through the dream and the process of the dream so we don't bail out.

3. The Roadblock of Selfishness - The Solution is Selflessness

Being selfish is something we are all born with. You don't have to teach a baby how to say, "Mine!" It just does. You don't have to teach a child to take something that doesn't belong to them. They just do. We are born with inherent selfishness. It's the curse of sin from which Jesus came to set us free. If we want to stay babies and children in our spiritual journey, then we stay in a world that revolves around us. I've been around way too many people who were building their world around themselves. If you truly love people then you will build your world to serve them.

James 1:14 NKJV
But each one is tempted when he is drawn away by his own desires and enticed.

We overcome selfishness by becoming selfless. Selflessness evolves in our lives by giving up our self-perceived rights, or what we think we deserve. The deceitfulness of selfishness is that we think we deserve far more than we do. Honestly, we deserve hell. Thankfully through Jesus we get heaven, but it's not what we deserve. Becoming selfless means we expand our work to serve people outside of ourselves and think of others before we think of ourselves. In our self-driven society this can be tough. It can start with paying for someone's lunch our giving up a spot in line or serving at a soup kitchen. Regardless, we become selfless by thinking of ourselves less.

4. The Roadblock of Fear - The Solution is Courage & Faith

Fear is one of the most powerful forces on earth. Fear of the unknown paralyzes people from stepping out into the call of God for their lives. Most people are afraid of living their dream. People are afraid of sacrifice. They are afraid of stepping into something new. It reminds me of when my kids were little. They didn't want to be alone in the dark. Night after night I would have to leave the door cracked or all the way open so they could relax and eventually fall asleep. They weren't really afraid of the dark — they were afraid of what they couldn't see. Their imaginations would come up with so many different scenarios that would cause them to be afraid. Many times this is what happens to us when we are about to step into our dream. We are paralyzed by fear because we have so many "What if?" scenarios that run through our minds. This is why we need to renew our minds to think about what could go right instead of what could go wrong!

II Timothy 1:7 NKJV
For God has not given us a spirit of fear, but of power and of love and of a sound mind.

Fear is actually a spirit and we have been given spiritual authority over it. The promise of God is that we have a sound mind and we can overcome fear! Overcoming fear will take stirring up courage and faith in our minds and our hearts. Sometimes it takes expressing these fears to someone close to us. Having people in our life that love and understand us is a great way to overcome fear. They have the ability to stir courage in us.

I still remember the moment I wanted to get saved. I was 7 years old and at a Lutheran Vacation Bible School. My mom was actually there with me that day. I have no idea what was being said, but I do remember I wanted to answer the altar call and give my life to Jesus. The problem was that this was a very traditional church with lots of pews and stained glass and a huge honkin' set of organ pipes. It was just way too overwhelming for me as a little kid. Plus no one else went down to the front so I'd be there all by myself – but I just knew I was supposed to go.

My mom must've had a sense as well because she leaned over and asked me if I wanted to go down there. I told her I did but I didn't want to go alone. She then looked me in the eye and reminded me of how much courage it took David to go down and fight Goliath. This was my favorite Bible story as a kid and we had just read it the day before so it was fresh on my mind. She told me that if David had the courage to walk down in the valley to battle the giant then I could have the courage to walk the aisle at 7 years old. I remember that day so clearly because it was the day I realized that I can do anything for Jesus. It just takes a step of faith and little bit of courage. Whenever fear tries to paralyze us from living our dream, we must remember that there's a ton of things that can go right. It's up to us to step out in faith and believe for God's best!

5. The Roadblock of Insecurity - The Solution is Security in God

Insecurity is something most people struggle with at some level. When you feel rejected or excluded or even straight up disrespected, you have the opportunity to internalize that. You can start to believe that you are not good enough. It happens to everyone at some stage in life. We must learn to recognize our insecurities and not just sit back and think that it will never change, that it's just a part of who we are and everyone else just needs to accept it. No, they don't and no, you don't! Insecurity can keep us from our dream and God's best! It is fear that you will be alone or that people won't accept you for some reason. It's putting your hope in people.

INSECURITY IS BIRTHED FROM THE FEAR OF MAN.

I was very insecure as a man and as a leader early on in ministry. I would go to conferences and events hoping that "Brother Wonderful" would recognize me, and that would make me feel included. If someone made a bad comment on social media, I'd try to fix it and see what I could do to make it better. I labored for years under the delusion that all these people in ministry and life had my back and were for my good. Well when everything fell apart and I was left with nothing, no marriage, no kids, no church, no ministry...all those people were gone too. My security had been stripped away from me. All the years I thought I was sowing into these relationships and now they were just gone! My security was gone too. It was a divine pruning. God had to cut away all the superficial stuff so he could get me to the place where my trust and security was in Him alone.

> **WE OVERCOME INSECURITY BY FINDING OUR SECURITY IN GOD AND GOD ALONE.**

If our security is in who we know or what we do, when that goes away we are left completely broken. This is why it is so important to find our identity, value, and worth in Jesus. This is why now I could care less what people think about me, if so-and-so invites me to their church, if Mr. Famous Preacher recognizes me... I could honestly give two craps about that. Yes, I said two craps. My security isn't found in the opinion and fear of man, it is found in the work of the brutal cross and miraculous resurrection of Jesus Christ. That's all that matters. Don't live your dream for anyone but an audience of One.

6. The Roadblock of Naïvety - The Solution is Wisdom

This was a big one for me. The definition of naïve is being trusting, simple or inexperienced. Being naïve isn't all bad. It is actually a very good characteristic to have because it is built on a foundation of trust. I used to be a very naïve person because I was brought up to take people at face value. Over the years though, I've been betrayed and taken of advantage of because of my trusting nature. It seems like that the closer you get to God the more trusting you become, unfortunately people will take advantage of this.

Matthew 5:8 NKJV
Blessed are the pure in heart, for they shall see God.

Being naturally naïve is ok, there's a purity in heart that comes with it. At some point you are going to have to trust other people because your dream depends on it. No one who has ever done anything great has done it by themselves. There are always people who will be there to help you and to hurt you. This is why we still remain pure and innocent but employ wisdom.

Matthew 10:16 NKJV
Behold, I send you out as sheep in the midst of wolves. Therefore be wise as serpents and harmless as doves.

James 1:5 NKJV
If any of you lacks wisdom, let him ask of God, who gives to all liberally and without reproach, and it will be given to him.

Being wise is a choice. If you are naïve like me, then it's imperative to use wisdom and surround yourself with people who have your best interest at heart. You know they have your best interest at heart by what they do, not by what they say. Don't give people titles and positions in your life or organization until they've earned it. I was so trusting in my first church plant that I just handed out positions and titles because I naturally thought everyone had my best interest at heart. Well needless to say, but I'm going to say it anyway...they didn't! I learned a very hard lesson. I gained wisdom through experience and I haven't made the same mistake since. You have to trust what people do, not what people say. If you are naïve, it's ok, just make sure to use wisdom before allowing every person with a compliment to come into your life and put their hands on your dream.

7. The Roadblock of Discouragement - The Solution is Encouragement & Self-Encouragement

One of the biggest roadblocks you will face in your dream is discouragement. To say it simply, it's when someone or something disses your courage, or disrespects what you're trying to do with your life and your dream. To take it a step further, you actually believe what they are saying rather than what God has said. Discouragement can de-motivate you quicker than anything else because it isn't what happened to you —it's what you believe happened to you. The biggest enemy is IN-A-ME. We are our own worst enemy when it comes to discouragement. We can't believe everything we think sometimes. We must get by this roadblock or it can keep us locked up on the journey to our dream for years!

We get through this roadblock by encouragement. Encouragement is fuel for the soul. The most valuable but yet inexpensive form of incentive is a word of encouragement. This why I love preachers who are encouraging. This is why I surround myself with people who are encouraging. If you aren't positive and encouraging, chances are you ain't hangin' with me! I've had way too many negative knuckleheads in my life! It's up to us to create an environment of encouragement. Sometimes we may find ourselves all alone and with no one around to encourage us, like I was years ago. This is when we start the task of encouraging ourselves like David did! This could be one of the saddest verses in the bible because he had no one to encourage him but we can learn from it!

Psalm 43:5 NIV
Why, my soul, are you downcast? Why so disturbed within me? Put your hope in God, for I will yet praise him, my Savior and my God.

In this particular psalm David is by himself. There is no beautiful keyboard, inviting altar call, or loving pastor around. He's in a cave with people trying to kill him! He had to speak to himself. You've got to tell yourself that you are mighty, that no weapon formed against you will prosper, that if God be for you then who can be against you?! This is when you dig into the word of God and start speaking the promises of God over yourself. The word of God is where eternal encouragement comes from! You don't have to live discouraged, make the choice to live in encouragement!

8. The Roadblock of Depression - The Solution is Joy

Depression. Just the word makes you feel sad. It's like being deflated, dejected, devalued, demotivated. Leaving you feeling less than. The roadblock of depression has derailed many people greater than you or me. It's a very real thing and shouldn't be taken lightly. It can happen through a circumstance or situation, it can happen through a chemical imbalance in our body, it can happen a number of different ways but regardless of how it happens, we must overcome this roadblock. Depression can lead us down a dangerous and disastrous road, leaving us thinking there is no hope or solution. Depression is not only real but a tactic of the enemy to leave us ineffective in living our God-given dream.

How do we overcome this roadblock? We can do all kinds of surface things to make us feel happy. The problem is, happiness is an emotion just like sadness is an emotion. Happiness and sadness can be determined by an exterior circumstance. Depression is a state of being, so the only way to overcome it is through the spiritual solution of JOY. Joy is not an emotion and it isn't something you can muster up. Joy is a fruit of the Spirit. It is a living thing that can be nurtured through a relationship with God. Having an attitude of thankfulness can grow this spiritual fruit. Thanking God for things you do have in your life, nurtures joy. Start by thanking God for the breath in your lungs. We all have something to be grateful for. The main thing is that Jesus died for our sins so we don't have to go to hell! That right there should stir us our of our funk.

Psalm 51:12 NIV
Restore to me the joy of your salvation and grant me a willing spirit, to sustain me.

Nehemiah 8:10 NIV
Nehemiah said, "Go and enjoy choice food and sweet drinks, and send some to those who have nothing prepared. This day is holy to our Lord. Do not grieve, for the joy of the Lord is your strength."

> **JOY IS A PERMANENT ATTITUDE THAT CAN OVERCOME ANYTHING LIFE THROWS OUR WAY.**

Keeping our joy is what keeps us strong. Depression can knock us down, but joy is what gets us up. Determine that no matter what happens to you, you are going to keep an attitude of joy!

9. The Roadblock of Hopelessness - The Solution is Faith

Hope is a powerful thing. They say that in prisoner camps the difference between the prisoners who make it and the ones who don't are in the daily routine of what they do. The prisoners who made it out alive ate well, they

they exercised, they shaved their faces, and lived as if they were going home very soon. The ones who gave up hope fell into depression, stopped taking care of themselves and had made up their minds they would die in that prisoner camp. So what kept the others alive? Hope and faith.

Hebrews 6:19 NIV
We have this hope as an anchor for the soul, firm and secure.

We must learn what it means to have hope as the anchor for our soul. Don't let go of hope. Hope is what wakes us up in the morning. Hope is what keeps us moving towards a better tomorrow. The solution to hopelessness is faith.

Hebrews 11:1 NKJV
Now faith is the substance of things hoped for, the evidence of things not seen.

Faith is the substance of hope! Hope is a wonderful thing but it is faith that makes hope real and eternal. Faith is what moves us towards action to make things right in our life and our relationships. Faith is what empowers our dream! Faith is the fuel to our future! Don't ever let a circumstance or a person take away your hope and your faith. This is vital to seeing your dream come to pass.

10. The Roadblock of Doubt & Negativity - The Solution is a Positive Outlook

Ever get around someone who is just always down and out? I love the Saturday Night Live sketch about Debbie Downer. I can so relate because no matter what environment or team I've been in or worked with, there's always one in the group. Having someone with constant negativity and doubt around you is like living next door to a toxic waste dump! Eventually you will get infected!

It also reminds me of the old Winnie the Pooh character, Eeyore. He was constantly speaking that negative things would probably happen. I know you can hear it now, "Probably rain today." It is a funny comparison but it is so true. We can't go around speaking all the negative things that are "probably" going to happen. Our words have power!

The tongue has the power of life and death, and those who love it will eat its fruit.
Proverbs 18:21 NIV

This is more than positive thinking, it's positive living! Having a positive outlook is imperative to living your God-given dream.

> **YOU HAVE TO WAKE UP EVERY DAY AND SPEAK POSITIVE THINGS OVER YOUR LIFE.**

This is why it's so important to memorize scripture, not to become a head full of knowledge but so that you can speak the word of God over your life and your future! Don't let someone dump negativity into your life. You have been redeemed from too much to just let anybody say whatever they want about you and your future!

Jesus died so that you could live the very best life for Him on this earth. Speaking positively about you, your family, and your future has more implications than you may ever realize. Words are seed that we sow into our futur. The seeds we sow will come back as a harvest at some level. It would be wise for us to practice the power of positive confession over our lives on a daily basis. Don't allow negativity to set itself in your life. Your dream is too important.

11. The Roadblock of Failure - The Solution is Determination

Failure and disillusionment can be one of the worst things anybody could ever experience. Failure has killed more dreams than anything else. As I mentioned earlier, when you drive by a cemetery you aren't just driving by people who have died and passed from this life to the next, you are probably driving by many dreams that died with them because of failure. Failure is an event. It's a momentary event that happens, it's not something that lives with you. It's not a state of mind. It's not a relationship, it's not a person. Failure can't rule your life, unless you let it. We must learn to fail forward. Learning from our failure is part of living our dream.

Let's think about Harland "Colonel" Sanders, the founder of Kentucky Fried Chicken. He lived in his car for 2 years and was rejected 1,009 times before finally finding a restaurant owner who agreed to use his secret chicken recipe. Here's a guy, aged 65, living in his car driving around the country looking for someone to buy his chicken recipe. He took over a thousand "No's" before getting even one "Yes". That's 1.4 'No's' per day every day for 2 years. By 1964, 9 years after he hit the road, his chicken was being sold in 600 restaurants in the US and Canada. Colonel Sanders eventually sold Kentucky Fried Chicken for $2 million.

Let's think about another chicken recipe entrepreneur – Truett Cathey, the founder of Chik-fil-A. After serving in the US Army during World War II, Truett and his brother opened the Dwarf House restaurant in 1946 in Atlanta, GA. Over the course of the next 20 years, his restaurant would burn down twice. Both times, he would go on to rebuild it. Could you imagine the heartbreak of watching everything you've built burn down not once, but twice?! Well, in November of 1967, the first Chick-fil-A restaurant opened in the Greenbriar Shopping Center in Atlanta, GA. Fast forward ahead to our current day and age, where Chick-fil-A is a national brand with gross revenues exceeding $4.5 billion a year, despite his mandate that each of the more 1600 fast food restaurants be closed on Sundays!

These two men didn't let failure stop them from succeeding. They had a determination that was bigger than their failure.

> **THERE IS LIFE BEYOND "NO!"**

I've found that many times rejection is God's way of protection or promotion. If you got everything you were actually hoping for, maybe in a failed job interview or a failed relationship, then you could have missed out on what God wants to do, which is give you bigger and better than you could imagine! Stay determined, stay in the fight, and don't let failure determine your course!

12. The Roadblock of Laziness - The Solution is Passion & Motivation

One of the classic comedies in our society is a movie called "Office Space." There's a scene when our beloved character Peter is just having a slow start to the work week and an overly enthusiastic co-worker walks up and says in a very awkward and super cheesy way, "Sounds like someone is having a case of the 'Mondays!'" This to me is the perfect picture of indifference, which is another form of laziness. What causes laziness is a lack of desire, a lack of passion and an overall complacency towards the task at hand. Unfortunately people can be like this with their own dream. Maybe they get beat up in life, maybe they have too much emotional baggage, maybe they just have given up, or maybe they really are having a case of the Mondays! Whatever it is it must be identified and overcome in order for the dream to be fulfilled.

> **I'D RATHER HAVE AN OUNCE OF PASSION THAN A POUND OF TALENT.**

There are many gifted and talented people who do nothing because they feel entitled based on their giftedness. It doesn't matter how gifted or talented you are, if you don't work hard and are passionately in love with what you do, then your dream will never become what it could be. There are times to rest and play, but there are times to work and you've got to work hard. The mojo happens when you are in your sweet spot of giftedness and you are passionate and you apply that through hard work. When that happens, you see the fullness of your calling on display for God's glory. It's an experience that is indescribable. You'll know it when you feel it! Understand this: if you aren't passionate about your dream then no one else will be either. In order to fulfill a dream bigger than yourself, it has to be an inspired vision. The passionate meter has to be on overflow! If your dream doesn't inspire you to work hard it probably won't inspire others to work hard either. Putting things off until tomorrow is not the answer. Every dreamer who's done great things has been a self-starter and did today what others put off until tomorrow.

Ecclesiastes 11:4 TLB
If you wait for perfect conditions, you will never get anything done.

We can't wait for everything to be in place before we make a big step in our dream. God responds to faith. Sometimes we're waiting on God to make everything perfect before we move, but sometimes God is waiting for us to step out and trust Him!

13. The Roadblock of Ignorance - The Solution is Knowledge

The old saying, "You don't know what you don't know" is simple but true! Most people won't become all that they could be simply because of their own self-imposed ignorance. I know that sounds harsh, but even more harsh is not educating yourself in order to reach your God-given dream. I've found over the years that education is important but educating yourself is invaluable. When you are passionate about something you will do whatever it takes to learn all you can about it. Knowledge is key in reaching your dreams. Educating yourself is something that no college course can teach you. In this day and age we have so many tools around us in order to get educated. We are inundated with information that can further our dreams. The issue is not ignorance due to a lack of information, it's ignorance due to a lack of obtaining that information! I read books, watch videos, go to conferences, and do as much research as I can to become all that God has in mind for me. I move towards the next step and actually apply this knowledge to my life.

Some folks think that wisdom and knowledge are the same thing. Unfortunately it's not the same. Wisdom and knowledge are very closely related but in fact very different. When we gain knowledge but don't use it, it's like filling your head with information that is useless. I imagine many people who have these big bobble heads full of knowledge but never use it! When we use wisdom we actually take what we've learned, knowledge, and apply it to our situation. That's the problem with most Christians, they ask for wisdom but are wondering where the knowledge is! It's on us to gain the knowledge, and then God will give us wisdom in order for us to make the right decision. So you, right now, reading this book is a perfect example of someone gaining the knowledge they need in order to apply wisdom to reach their God-given dream.

14. The Roadblock of Inconvenience & Uncomfortability - The Solution is Sacrifice

Your dream is going to cost you more than you thought, it's going to take more time than you anticipated, and it may even cost you some dear relationships. Sometimes the people that were with you in one season just can't go with you into the next. Either you'll outgrow them or they'll outgrow you, but regardless it will cost you. Your dream isn't going to just fall into your lap. It's going to take sacrifice and a lot of inconvenient moments. I know we don't like to hear about being inconvenienced because our society is built around us being serviced for ease. Well newsflash! Your dream won't be easy. Joseph's dream journey was difficult and filled with so many "inconvenient" moments to say the least

The reality is that more often than not we will be uncomfortable in living our dream. We will be uncomfortable but comfort isn't the goal. Most people live life from a zone of comfort. The problem is, God lives outside of comfort zones. When Jesus saved humanity from the curse of death and sin, He wasn't comfortable! If we are to follow our Savior into discipleship then we have to get off of this idea that we are to be comfortable every second of every day of our life! The principle here is called, "Pay Now & Play Later." If we pay the price of sacrifice now we can play in the success of our efforts tomorrow. Anybody who is experiencing the fullness of God's blessing today can tell you that their yesterdays were filled with sacrifice. Now understand this: it's so totally worth it! Your dream is worth it. You are worth it! Your comfort is worth the great dream on your life.

15. The Roadblock of Poverty & Greed - The Solution is Prosperity & Generosity

Sometimes we can get so caught up in our dream that we become selfish and we feel that the dream is all about us. Joseph understood his dream was about helping others. That selfishness we start to engage in makes us small in our thinking and we can develop a scarcity mentality. A scarcity mentality thinks we won't have enough or we have to be protective of what we have. We can become greedy. Greed is selfishness' slimy cousin. I've found that greedy people are highly insecure people. Not insecure about their looks or whatever, but truly insecure, meaning NOT secure in the fact that God will meet their needs. Greed has a way of blinding people to the truth, even if it's right in front of their face. I have had the experience of watching what happens to someone when they rely on people to meet their needs instead of God. It becomes a sad, shallow show indeed. I've also found that greed leads to poverty. There's a difference between being wise with your finances and being greedy. Most poverty that someone experiences is birthed out of greed. I've never seen a happy, joyous and free person who was greedy. Remember, poverty has nothing to do with money, it has everything to do with the state of your heart, the mindset you have about money, and the attitude you have about your situation. Living rich isn't about your wallet, it's about being rich in life and relationships. The antidote is generosity. Generosity will clear the roadblock of greed out of your life.

> **SOME PEOPLE ARE SO POOR ALL THEY HAVE IS MONEY!**

Philippians 4:19 NKJV
And my God shall supply all your need according to His riches in glory by Christ Jesus.

This is why it's so important to start the process of becoming a giver. For me, it started with tithing at my local church. Tithing is the biblical path toward generosity. Tithing isn't some mystical thing, it's what gets us into the habit of becoming generous. It's when we give not just any 10% of our income to the local church, but when we give the first 10% to our local church. It's making generosity a priority. Through our giving we are making sure that we honor God as the giver of every blessing we experience in life. Tithing shouldn't be legalistic and religious, it should be done with joy. If we tithe with joy then we will be able to give in other situations with joy as well. Becoming a generous person will be vital to seeing your dream come true. You don't have to be rich to be generous, you just have to start with what you have right now.

16. The Roadblock of Inaccuracy - The Solution is Clarity

Some people I meet and talk with about their dream seem to have Dream ADHD. It's like they have so many ideas they want to pursue and they aren't really sure which idea is a part of their dream and which dream for their life is actually from God. So it begs the question, is this dream yours or God's? Is this dream all about you or is it about God's purpose for your life? If our dream is all about us then it is too small. Our dream should be crystal clear and based on God's redemptive purpose for the earth. Jesus saving people is where our dream needs to be based.

Matthew 28:18-20 NIV
Then Jesus came to them and said, "All authority in heaven and on earth has been given to me. Therefore go and make disciples of all nations, baptizing them in the name of the Father and of the Son and of the Holy Spirit, and teaching them to obey everything I have commanded you. And surely I am with you always, to the very end of the age."

This passage of scripture is known as the Great Commission. This is God's dream. The Great Commission is God's dream for everyone. Our specific skill set and gifting is where that fits in. Our dream should have eternal implications for the lives of people around us. When we get really clear on our dream then we have the power to fulfill that dream. Our purpose produces clarity. We cannot get into having a divided focus. A divided focus happens when our motives are out of whack.

Are we motivated by money, opportunity, power, pride? What is it that motivates us to chase our dream? The answer to this question will bring clarity.

WRAPPING UP

In closing this chapter, we can see that roadblocks will happen in our dream process, but God has given us every tool and weapon we need to fight for and build the dream He has put in our hearts. Every person who has lived their dream has overcome adversity. One of the most amazing and beautiful things about God is that He cares for us just as a good Father would. God doesn't make bad things happen to us so we will learn a lesson. I'm not trying to explain how God works but I do know, it's not like that. I guess, I'm simply saying that He is God and we aren't going to understand why things happen. He asks us to trust Him. Trust and understanding are two completely different things. I trust Him as a good Father and I know He has nothing but good things for me. I may not understand why I'm going through something, but I do know I won't be alone. I do know that God has empowered me and I do know He loves me. So with that in mind, I can walk through anything… and so can you!

CHAPTER 6

Stewarding the Dream

STEWARDING THE DREAM

I love the term "stewarding" because it implies that I'm not really the owner of anything. Stewarding means that Someone else owns it but it has been entrusted to me as a manager. This is the principle found all throughout the kingdom of God. God is the owner and I am the steward. The owner is always checking on our progress, always challenging us to do better with what He has provided. Many people waste what they have been entrusted with while other people increase what has been entrusted to them. We've been entrusted with relationships, careers, finances, organizations, and the list goes on and on. When we get in the mindset that God has entrusted a dream for us to steward then it becomes more serious for us to make the dream happen, because we are working for the Lord and not just ourselves. This is when we realize the dream is bigger than us.

Proverbs 29:18 NKJV
Where there is no vision, the people perish:

Proverbs 29:18 NIV
Where there is no revelation, people cast off restraint;

Without vision people perish or cast off restraint. A dream and a vision will build certain parameters and limitations into your life. When you have a dream there are certain things you will and won't be able to do according to the specificity of your dream. For instance, if my dream is to pastor a thriving church then I can't go out partying every Saturday night. It just won't work for the dream. If your dream is to be a gold medal track star at the Olympics then eating that Oreo probably isn't going to help you. The dream comes with self-imposed limitations that will actually help us get there faster, but it's up to us to put those boundaries in place.

I remember when I first received the call of ministry back in the 90's and everything changed in my life. It was this principle that kept me close to Jesus. I strayed away for sure from time to time but ultimately it was the vision and the dream He had put in my life that helped me stay focused and on track. I had and still have a vision of being an influential church leader with a powerful and thriving church. That type of vision is going to come with things that I can and cannot do. I can't hang out with the same people. I can't hang out at the same places. I have to build new relationships and find new places to invest my time in. A vision and a dream is a powerful thing. It can help drive you and keep you focused.

STEWARDING THE DREAM OF ANOTHER

The seeds of a dream are being planted all throughout your life. God is equipping you for the dream He has for you even when we don't realize it. Usually when we are serving the dream of someone else, we are coming closer to living His dream for us. God will give us a divine strategy for seeing our dreams come true, and it's usually through helping another person's dream come to pass. When we are generous with our time, our resources, and our relationships, God uses those things to help us fulfill the dreams of other people.

Maybe in life our dream should be helping others fulfill their dreams. Maybe our call is to be a dream-maker. Being a dream-maker means that you are open with your life. If you hear of a need from someone you believe in, help meet that need. I've found that God will place dream-makers in my life after I've become a dream-maker in the life of someone else. Dream-makers have a strategic network of like-minded and authentic relationships. I have several friends that have helped me immensely through the course of my life. Through the darkest seasons when I had nothing to offer, these guys surrounded me and helped make my dreams happen. I fully believe that happened because I spent hours upon hours on the phone with other pastors and church planters consulting and freely pouring into these men of God in order that they would be encouraged personally and that they would grow their churches all across the nation.

We must also be dream encouragers. Dream encouragers are people who may not have the connections or resources to make a dream happen, but they have words, thoughts, and prayers. Encouragement is the most inexpensive form of motivation because it's free! Encouraging the dream of another person is like rocket fuel for their soul. I've found that when someone encourages us in our dream it gives us a fire to keep going forward even in the most uncertain situations. On a similar note, I found that criticism in our dream can make the realization of that dream all the more harder. When you have someone in your corner, cheering you on in the fulfillment of your dream, it comes with encouragement, accountability, and a new sense of determination. The best way to experience our dreams is to help others reach theirs. Check out these tips on encouraging the dreams of others.

- **Encourage the person and the dream.**

The point is people. When we encourage people in their gifts and abilities it adds value to them. This is our goal, adding value to others. If they are truly walking out a God-given dream then encouragement is going to be vital to the process. Sometimes people can't just encourage themselves all the time — they need you to do it! There have been more times than I can count that someone will encourage me through a text or a call and it just helped me stay the course and not get frustrated in the process.

- **Be a helper not a hindrance.**

Building someone else's dream isn't about building their dream for them, it's about contributing what you can. It may be finances, a person they need to meet, or anything that you have to offer. Whatever it is, make sure it's a help and not a hindrance. Being a helper sometimes comes with keeping opinions to ourselves. We may think that they should do this or that but we must realize that it's their dream and not ours! We can offer advice when it is asked for but let's not try and alter what someone is called to do. We are there to love, support, and encourage. This is how we can help.

- **Be a dream-builder not a dream-breaker.**

This is key. Some of us have a tendency to be negative, making sure to come up with reasons why another person's dream will succeed instead of voicing the reasons why it could fail. Sometimes a dream is all a person has. Our words carry weight and have power. Jesus said that we will be accountable to every idle word we speak. How much more powerful the words we speak to others about their God-given dream. We must use our words to help build the dream of another instead of breaking them down.

BUILDING THE DREAM OF ANOTHER

Luke 16:12 NKJV
And if you have not been faithful in what is another man's, who will give you what is your own?

This whole chapter in Luke is mind-blowing when we really think about it. It's all about stewardship. Stewardship is key in reaching your dream. We must steward everything around us in a way that is careful and diligent because the Master is coming back for it. How did we steward our time here on earth? How did we steward our family? How did we steward the relationships in our life? How did we steward the financial blessing God gave us? How did we steward this great dream that He's entrusted to us?

This is why I love the story of Joseph. He had a dream when he was young. He had zero capability to pull this dream off. He had zero connections, zero experience. Joseph shouldn't have succeeded at the end of his life – but he did. Joseph discovered a principle that many successful people have practiced for centuries. It's through the supernatural process of helping, building, stewarding, giving, and sacrificing for the dream of another that your dreams come to complete fruition. I can't explain how, but I do know that it works. I've experienced it time and time again. When I invest into people, even people who do me wrong – actually, especially when people do me wrong – I still receive the supernatural blessing of God!

The first thing we need to understand is it's all Pharaoh's dream right now. Meaning that Pharaoh had a massive dream that God had called Joseph to steward. Even though, Joseph had a dream as a kid but Pharaoh's dream is what matters most right now. It's just like you. Your dream matters but right now someone else's dream probably needs your attention. It was Pharaoh's dream but it was Joseph's ability to pull it off. God will place you in environments in which He will use the gift and years of training and experience in order for you to steward the dream of another.

Let's deconstruct the process here a bit through the text we've been discussing. Here are five things I've found when stewarding and building the dream of another.

1. God will place a leader in your life with a great dream.

Genesis 41:1-7 NKJV
When two full years had passed, Pharaoh had a dream: He was standing by the Nile, when out of the river there came up seven cows, sleek and fat, and they grazed among the reeds. After them, seven other cows, ugly and gaunt, came up out of the Nile and stood beside those on the riverbank. And the cows that were ugly and gaunt ate up the seven sleek, fat cows. Then Pharaoh woke up. He fell asleep again and had a second dream: Seven heads of grain, healthy and good, were growing on a single stalk. After them, seven other heads of grain sprouted—thin and scorched by the east wind. The thin heads of grain swallowed up the seven healthy, full heads. Then Pharaoh woke up; it had been a dream.

I remember when I first got into ministry full-time. I was just starting out in California as a youth pastor when on my first day in the office, one of our elders let me know I had a new computer with all the latest applications. Man! I was so excited. He also let me know he had installed Photoshop 7 just in case I may want to mess around with it. Well, if you know anything about Photoshop, it's come a long way from

Photoshop 7! Now that I think about it, that decision he made impacted the rest of my life. Not only did I mess around with Photoshop a little, I ended up getting pretty good at it! I started to discover a gift on my life that I didn't know I really had.

> **THE MOMENT YOU SAY, "YES" TO GOD BY SERVING ANOTHER PERSON'S DREAM IS THE MOMENT GOD MAY UNLEASH A GIFT ON YOUR LIFE THAT WILL HELP BUILD YOUR OWN DREAM.**

The moment I said yes to trying out graphic design is the moment God unleashed this gift on my life. It was the gift of communication, but it was to communicate the gospel visually. As mentioned before, this gift has opened doors to so many opportunities that have helped finance my life and continue to expand influence throughout the kingdom of God. This gift continues to be a blessing to me and countless other church leaders across the nation because I'm able to help local churches reach more people through visual communication. But it all started by saying, "Yes" to the leader God placed in my life. Sometimes God is just waiting for us to be willing. I didn't really even have the ability but I had the availability and then God increased the gift. I had no idea how this gift would be employed but here I am years later with a church of my own being able to employ those early lessons of church creativity in an environment God has trusted me with to steward. It was through saying, "Yes" and building this man's dream that God brought me to the next level of my destiny and purpose here on earth!

2. God will make sure He positions people in the right place at the right time.

Genesis 41:8-13 NKJV
In the morning his mind was troubled, so he sent for all the magicians and wise men of Egypt. Pharaoh told them his dreams, but no one could interpret them for him. Then the chief cupbearer said to Pharaoh, "Today I am reminded of my shortcomings. Pharaoh was once angry with his servants, and he imprisoned me and the chief baker in the house of the captain of the guard. Each of us had a dream the same night, and each dream had a meaning of its own. Now a young Hebrew was there with us, a servant of the captain of the guard. We told him our dreams, and he interpreted them for us, giving each man the interpretation of his dream. And things turned out exactly as he interpreted them to us: I was restored to my position, and the other man was impaled."

I just love this passage of scripture. If you go back and read this story, Joseph had asked this guy two years ago to put a good word in for him! Two years! I wonder if Joseph was thinking, "I mean seriously dude, I've been sitting in this jail cell for two more years and now you bring my name up?! What gives?!" Well maybe not, maybe that's what I'd be thinking. In reality, God was still working in Joseph that extra two years. Maybe that's where you are, you've been waiting and waiting. Well, keep waiting!

God is going to remind people about you. This is why it is so important to keep your relationships in the best standing possible. Let's be real, you won't be able to please everybody, you won't be friends with everybody, and there are some people who will actually endeavor to misunderstand you and not like you for any reason. It is up to us to keep the bridges polished and clean.

> **SO MANY PEOPLE ARE QUICK TO BURN A BRIDGE, BUT IF YOUR LIFE IS FILLED WITH BURNED BRIDGES YOU BECOME AN ISLAND TO YOURSELF!**

Isolation is one of the worst places you can be when it comes to the kingdom of God. We need each other. So if at all possible, stay in good standing with the relationships you have and reach out to start new ones as well.

When it comes to the kingdom, I've found things are backwards from the way society tries to educate us. In society, they teach you that it's all about you, you've got to crush people on your way to the top, you've got to look out for yourself, and the same type of rhetoric that goes with being successful in this day and age. The interesting thing about the kingdom is that in order to be first you must be last and in order to receive you must be humble. Our society has taught us to rely on ourselves but the kingdom teaches us to rely solely on God. Please understand, you don't have to push your way through or forward. In this dog eat dog world God will make sure there are no dogs around! God is your defender, even more your Father. He completely understands what you need and when you need it.

I can't tell you how many times an old relationship has come back around and been beneficial to me and not even because I tried! It amazes me the people that God will use to connect us with that next opportunity. It comes through healthy, authentic relationships; relationships with no other motive than to love the other person and to be a help to them. We must make sure to nurture the relationships in our life. They could be the key to our destiny later in life. They just may be who God uses to open that door for you!

3. Be prepared when your opportunity comes.

Genesis 41:14 NKJV
So Pharaoh sent for Joseph, and he was quickly brought from the dungeon. When he had shaved and changed his clothes, he came before Pharaoh.

Sometimes we aren't fully prepared spiritually, physically, emotionally, or mentally. As I read the scripture above, something intriguing stuck out to me. It says, "When he had shaved and changed his clothes." The Holy Spirit allowed this to be in the scriptures for a reason. I believe the reason is to show us the importance of preparation. Think about it; Pharaoh knew Joseph was in prison, he knew Joseph probably had a big 'ole beard, tattered clothes and stunk to high heaven! So Pharaoh probably didn't expect Joseph to be showered, clean shaven, and in new clothes, but Joseph was prepared. He knew that his appearance may affect how Pharaoh would receive him.

How people perceive you is how they receive you. Joseph understood this principle because he took the time to get prepared physically before he stepped into what God had for him. Also, through the years of adversity Joseph was prepared emotionally to handle what God had waiting for him. He was betrayed by his own family! Of course by this time in his life he knew how to master his emotions.

Think about all the positions Joseph served in. They all had pretty important responsibilities, from overseeing people to strategizing systems to day in and day out operations. Joseph was a smart guy. He prepared himself mentally as well. So how about spiritually? Are we prepared spiritually to step into what God has for us? We'll talk about that in the next point.

PREPARATION PRECEDES ADVANCEMENT.

As Christ-followers we should be constantly be improving ourselves through continual learning. I'm a big fan of conferences, books, podcasts, and blogs. Think about what could happen if we read one book a month on an area in which we are gifted. In one year that's twelve books. Wow! That's like a masterclass! This is how experts become experts. This is how good leaders become great leaders. This is how people go to the next level in their finances. They are learning and applying, but they are doing it in the area where they are gifted. A rolling stone gathers no moss! We should constantly be hungry for more of God's revelation.

I travel quite a bit and preach a lot of this message you are reading right now. It's inevitable that someone will come up to me and tell me how inspired they were and how they want to run after their dream. I'll ask, "Well, what do you sense God is telling you to do? What's your dream?"

I've heard some good ones. This next story is exaggerated a bit to make the point, but I do remember a conversation very similar to this next one.

Someone once said, "I want to be the next real-estate mogul. I'll make a kajillion dollars and give it all to the church!"

Me: Ok… awesome. Let's ask some questions here. Have you received your real-estate license?

Him: No. But I'm a good man, I'm gonna be the next big real estate mogul, you'll see!

Me: So, have you taken any classes about real estate?

Him: No, but I've seen it on TV man, it's easy!

Me: Have you read any books on real estate?

Him: No… but God will guide me!

Me: <blank stare>

Think about how silly that is. Obviously that is a bit of a fictional conversation but hopefully, you get the point. If we have a great dream and we are gifted by God to make that dream happen, then we must be ready to enter many seasons of preparation. We must be willing to work hard and do our part and then watch God do His part.

Ultimately, here's what we need to understand: God is sovereign and infinite and He is wisdom. He knows exactly what we need before we need it. The world we live in is a pretty remarkable place with some pretty remarkable people in it. I think about the single mom who has a disabled child, a son who sits by the bedside of a parent who has cancer, parents who lose a child too soon. I think about some of these impossible situations and wonder how they get through it. How do they do it? Grace. God's grace carries them through these dark places. You don't really know what God has done in you until it's time to use it, then all of a sudden you realize God has been preparing you your whole life for this moment!

> **WHEN YOU ARE IN A TOUGH SITUATION YOU MUST REALIZE THAT GOD HAS PREPARED YOU FOR IT.**

4. When opportunity knocks, remember to give God glory.

Genesis 41:15-16 NKJV
Pharaoh said to Joseph, "I had a dream, and no one can interpret it. But I have heard it said of you that when you hear a dream you can interpret it." "I cannot do it," Joseph replied to Pharaoh, "but God will give Pharaoh the answer he desires."

This is where the proof of Joseph's spiritual preparation was tested. By his answer, he showed that he knew it was God's gift on his life for God's glory. There were things that God needed to do in Joseph. While God doesn't make bad things happen to people, He does allow circumstances. Through these circumstances we can learn and develop and grow, or we can become bitter, sour, and angry. Joseph chose to grow, he chose to serve, he chose to steward Pharaoh's dream and God blessed Joseph through it all. Not only did he favor and protect Joseph, but He also prepared him for his destiny. I love how this scripture is laid out in context. Pharaoh asked if Joseph can do it and Joseph tells him no. Pharaoh must have thought, "Then why are you standing here in front of me?" It's kinda comical but Joseph really wanted make it clear, that it was God's gift on his life for God's glory. Sometimes we get all up in our ego and believe our own hype like we are something great. We must remember that God has created us and He in His sovereignty has blessed us with gifts, talents, and abilities. It's God's gift on our life for His glory. It's ok to hear, "thank you," but make sure that you aren't receiving something from that praise that you shouldn't be. Don't receive your security or self-worth or validation from the praise of people. People praised Jesus one day, then a few days later wanted him crucified! So it's imperative that we look to God in thankfulness for the gift that He has put on our life and receive our validation from the death, burial, and resurrection of Jesus! He loved us so much that He died so that we can experience the supernatural flow of grace and gifting right now, at this very moment.

5. Do the job right!

Genesis 41:25 NKJV
Then Joseph said to Pharaoh, "The dreams of Pharaoh are one and the same. God has revealed to Pharaoh what he is about to do.

Genesis 41:29-30 NKJV
Seven years of great abundance are coming throughout the land of Egypt, but seven years of famine will follow them. Then all the abundance in Egypt will be forgotten, and the famine will ravage the land.

This is the amazing part where God's gift flows through your life, and you make life-giving transformation happen for you and those in your world. Joseph had confidence in the gift on his life. Having confidence in the gift isn't enough though, you have to have faith in God and a sobering realization that this gift is actually just on loan and I'll need to give account for it at the end of my life.

It's unfortunate to see people get an amazing opportunity, but then it's not even anything on the outside that ruins it. It's actually self-sabotage because your character has to keep you where your gift takes you. I've been there! I've self-sabotaged a few major opportunities because I had things in my life that where unresolved and then I made some really bad choices to try and numb the symptoms of a much deeper problem. At a root level, God had to pull things up and rebuild. This is God's grace on all our lives. He will keep giving us opportunities, but it is up to us to make sure we can handle the blessing that comes with it. When the opportunity arises make sure to do it right and do it with integrity!

Colossians 3:23-24 NKJV
And whatever you do, do it heartily, as to the Lord and not to men, knowing that from the Lord you will receive the reward of the inheritance; for you serve the Lord Christ.

When we work, we are working for the Lord. This helps keep us on track for decisions throughout the day. It helps keep our mind focused on God and not on those around us. It helps keep our temptations at a minimum as well because at the core of who we really are, we really want to please God. When we work with this in mind, we keep an attitude of excellence. Excellence is an attitude and can be applied at any level of any organization. Excellence requires zero talent. Excellence doesn't need a budget. Excellence is built into every organizational culture through example. People who are excellent inspire other people to be excellent.

So what is excellence? Well, let's talk about what is NOT excellence. Excellence is not perfection. Perfection demands that nothing be out of place and no one does anything wrong. Already by that standard we can see that perfection is impossible. The only perfect thing is Jesus and our salvation through His perfect sacrifice. That is the standard! So perfection isn't the goal because it is unachievable. Excellence is the goal. Excellence is doing the best with what you have.

6. Position Yourself for Greatness

Genesis 41:33-40 NKJV
"And now let Pharaoh look for a discerning and wise man and put him in charge of the land of Egypt. Let Pharaoh appoint commissioners over the land to take a fifth of the harvest of Egypt during the seven years of abundance. They should collect all the food of these good years that are coming and store up the grain under the authority of Pharaoh, to be kept in the cities for food. This food should be held in reserve for the country, to be used during the seven years of famine that will come upon Egypt, so that the country may not be ruined by the famine." The plan seemed good to Pharaoh and to all his officials. So Pharaoh asked them, "Can we find anyone like this man, one in whom is the spirit of God?" Then Pharaoh said to Joseph, "Since God has made all this known to you, there is no one so discerning and wise as you. You shall be in charge of my palace, and all my people are to submit to your orders. Only with respect to the throne will I be greater than you."

Here is where the years of adversity, pain, and turmoil start to show how Joseph's character and wisdom has been developed. Many times we wonder, "Why is all this happening to me?" when the real question is "What is all this creating in me?" The years of imprisonment, humiliation, being overlooked, falsely accused, and taken advantage of had created in Joseph a solid, strong, unyielding character. It's like when water shapes a rock over years and years of pressure and this beautiful rock formation is something we all look at in awe. I hope you see yourself in this. The years of stress and pressure is shaping something beautiful in you!

> **PEOPLE WILL BE IN AWE AT THE FORMATION OF YOUR CHARACTER AND YOUR LIFE.**

This is where Joseph found himself. He struggled with this stuff for years I'm sure, and all the while knowing God had given him a dream for his life. This moment in scripture is something we should all note of. This is the moment where God has plucked Joseph up and set him on the first step to the next level. This can happen to all of us! You may be grappling with the understanding of why things are happening but you have to take courage, it is creating in you something you couldn't create yourself.

Let's look at this passage of scripture more closely. Joseph was very wise at this point. He realized this was his moment. This was the opportunity for him to take all of the years of training, management, and leadership and put it to use. The first three verses in this passage will change the trajectory of Joseph's life forever. In verses through 33-36 he lays out the plan and strategy for the dream. He then goes on to set himself up for success through positioning himself. The verse says, "let Pharaoh look for a discerning and wise man." Who was speaking at the time? Joseph! Joseph was talking about himself. He just put it out there and in verse 38 Pharaoh asked, "Who is this guy? Where can we find him?" Joseph's thinking to himself, "Who has two thumbs and a plan? THIS GUY!" Ha! Of course it's funny to picture that, but God placed Joseph there for His purpose and Joseph saw the opportunity and made it happen.

It wasn't that Joseph wanted to be something great. It just happened to turn out that way because that is how God does things. Joseph just wanted out of prison and wanted to see his dream come to pass. So he positioned himself for greatness. Positioning yourself for greatness is NOT going to every conference and trying to schmooze with the big names. Positioning yourself for greatness is NOT cutting people down to make yourself look better. Positioning yourself through greatness is NOT using people to build your thing. We position ourselves for greatness through SERVING. Jesus said, "The first will be last." Our way to greatness is serving. When we serve our family, our church, and those around us, we get our minds off of ourselves. The most selfish people are the ones who aren't serving and are consumed with their own interests.

Joseph had his own dream, but it was by building and stewarding the dream of another man that his dream came to pass. If you read in the later chapters, Joseph experienced not only his dream but full restoration of his family! This is how God does it. He doesn't just make your dream come to pass but he fills that dream with hope, love, restoration, and everything that God promises when it comes to a life restored.

The interesting thing about this entire story is that Pharaoh was not a good man. He considered himself a god. He didn't even believe in the God that Joseph served! He was a pagan who worshiped other pagan gods. So think about this, God still positioned Joseph under this man. The one true God positioned His servant Joseph under an idol-worshipping pagan leader. Why would God do that? Why wouldn't God put Joseph under a leader who was awesome and loved God? Well I've found, God will sometimes place you under a leader that is bad in order to work in you what needs to be healed, grown, or matured. The leader you're under may be a terrible leader and even kinda shady but regardless, that's where God has placed you for this season. You may be in a position on a church staff, in a job, or in some relationship where the leader doesn't do what leaders should do. It doesn't matter. You aren't serving that leader, you are serving God. This is the secret to keeping your heart right when it comes to serving bad leadership. That leader didn't call you or even place you where are right now. God did. God called Joseph just like He's calling you, so don't you dare throw in the towel or give up on God's call and dream for your life!

THE DANGER OF A BORROWED DREAM

I remember when God first called me into ministry. I had a pretty crazy couple of years leading up to my conversion but I still remember it like it was yesterday. From the moment I heard that voice in my heart telling me that I would preach like my youth pastor was doing, I had the choice to follow God's plan for my life or follow "man's ministry plan" for my life. God is my Father and He knows what I need, but plenty of people will try and tell you what you need to do. Now don't get me wrong, be humble, be teachable, but don't allow someone else's plan for your life to interfere with God's plan for your life!

God has a dream for us, but sometimes we want to take the same path as those who've gone before us. The problem is, there are no road signs in the desert! You have to follow God! Sometimes the appeal of someone else's dream is so great, we think that maybe that's our dream and what we are supposed to be doing. The problem with this is that God has a unique and individualized plan and dream and purpose for all of us that is personal just to us. Someone else's life and dream can be appealing and that's ok, but don't latch on to their dream thinking it's yours! Their dream can inspire you and that's about where it needs to end! I follow and watch and see what others are doing, but for me, I know where I'm headed.

So let's ask the important question then let's ask a few to help us bring clarity.

HOW DO YOU KNOW IF YOU HAVE A BORROWED DREAM?

1. Are you comparing your dream to someone else's?

Comparison is a killer of creativity and your own dream. If you are constantly looking at social media to try and see if your life, ministry, job, or whatever is a good as or better than someone else's, then you are caught in the trap of comparison. Everything you see on social media is not reality! Those images and video and whatever else you see is what people want you to see! You aren't going to see the years of pain or the struggle of sin or the criticism of others. You are only going to see the good stuff. Remember, practice is great but, we all like the highlight reel. The only competition and comparison we should be making is against ourselves. We are our toughest and truly, our only competition.

2. Does your dream fit your passion and where you are called?

For years I struggled with this. I have a dream of leading a great church that influences the world for Jesus and doing it in a creative, relevant way. When I was just straight doing graphic design I would find myself becoming increasingly frustrated. The frustration existed because I wasn't building the dream I felt God had put in my heart. Or was I? I wasn't necessarily passionate about graphic design, but I was passionate about creatively communicating the gospel. Looking back now, I can see that it was part of the process of the dream. I've saved so much money on web designers, graphic designers, social media strategists, video editors... all because I was faithful in the process of God. Am I still building a great church? Yes, but I'm doing it in a way that is specific to the way I'm wired. It's the same for you, you are on the track God needs you on in order to build in you the character to handle the dream.

Your dream is usually connected to a geographical location. New York is mostly known for finance, Los Angeles is movies and entertainment, Nashville is music and recording, and the list goes on and on. Your dream will be relevant to its location. Your dream has geographical significance. The soil of your habitation is where you will plant the seeds of your dream. That's why I love church planting because every city in every country needs a local church. The leaders of those local churches can be as versatile and different as fingerprints on your hand but the mission is still the same, to be co-laborers in the kingdom of God. Your dream is going to be specific to you. God has tailored you different from everybody else.

3. Does your dream benefit just you or everyone around you?

This is vital to the foundation of your dream. Jesus said to build our life on the rock, the firm foundation. It's true with your dream as well. The sinking sand of self is where most people start building their dream and it's why most dreams don't ever come to pass. It was built on the wrong foundation. I've said this before but it bears repeating. If your dream is just about you, it's too small. A God-sized dream requires a lot of people to be involved. The dream needs to have mutual benefits for everyone. If it's a borrowed dream then it's just about what you can gain.

The danger we can get into is interpreting someone else's dream and then taking their personal dream and trying to make it our own. We start to dress like them, act like them, and it's as if we take on their whole persona because we are so in love with the dream God gave them. Let me pause. I believe our success is in helping others build their dream, so there must be some level of ownership we take to help others reach their dreams. When we take it on as our own personal mandate and purpose for life then we get into the danger of a borrowed dream rather than the specific, individual cause and dream God has purposed for all of us.

GETTING IT RIGHT

Genesis 40:5 NKJV
Then the butler and the baker of the king of Egypt, who were confined in the prison, had a dream, both of them, each man's dream in one night and each man's dream with its own interpretation.

Here are three men who have a dream. The butler, the baker, and Joseph all have unique and individual dreams. Joseph will encounter a fourth man, being Pharaoh; and he will have a dream that will impact a lot of people. Notice that they all have a dream regardless of where they were in life. Every person has a dream and everyone has their own interpretation. The challenge is getting the interpretation right. Again, sometimes we get so caught up in someone else's dream that it makes it hard for us to interpret what God has for our own lives.

HOW DO WE GET THE INTERPRETATION RIGHT?

Here are 3 ways we can get the interpretation about our dreams correct.

1. Hear from God

Having a time that is completely dedicated to reading God's word, personal worship, and just taking the time to listen and pray. For me, this is a cup of strong coffee on my porch every morning. I've never received an audible word from God. I don't really expect to because God has said quite a bit in His word. I've learned that God's voice will never disagree with what's been written in His word! So I align my thoughts and motives with God's word. Then I look at what I feel, is God's dream for me, and I look at my individualized gifts, talent, and experiences. All of those combined help me make sure that I'm building the dream God has for me. This is vital to knowing that you are living God's dream for your life and not someone else's.

2. Test the Motive

If the dream is all about us, if it's a selfish dream. It's not from God. If it is to encourage build and help others, there's a good chance it is a God-given dream. God wouldn't give us a bigger dream than He gave Jesus. Jesus' dream was to redeem mankind from the curse of death, hell, and the grave, and that we would go into all the world and make disciples baptizing them in the name of the Father, Son, and Holy Spirit. So we need to understand that our dream should always point back to helping mankind and furthermore, getting them in relationship with God.

3. Have Compassion and Grace

Genesis 40:6-7 NKJV
And Joseph came in to them in the morning and looked at them, and saw that they were sad. So he asked Pharaoh's officers who were with him in the custody of his lord's house, saying, "Why do you look so sad today?"

Joseph noticed the butler and the baker in prison with him and actually took an interest in them. Think about Joseph's situation, he was in prison for a crime he didn't commit, but he took notice of two other guys and had compassion for them and actually had the grace to inquire about their emotional condition. He cared.

> **SOMETIMES ALL PEOPLE NEED FROM US IS THAT WE CARE; THAT WE TAKE THE TIME TO LISTEN TO THEM AND THEIR DREAM.**

Genesis 40:8 NKJV

And they said to him, "We each have had a dream, and there is no interpreter of it." So Joseph said to them, "Do not interpretations belong to God? Tell them to me, please."

One of the reasons Joseph was so successful throughout his dream journey is because he was generous with his gift. He had the ability and the compassion to listen to other people and interpret their dreams. We remember what happened when Joseph tried to barter his gift for his freedom. He stayed in prison another two years! This is one of the major keys to seeing your dream come to pass.

CHAPTER 7

The Realization of the Dream

THE REALIZATION OF THE DREAM

Walt Disney was turned down 302 times trying to get financed for Disney World. The Walt Disney company in 2014 was said to be worth over $48 billion… with a "b", billion.

Michael Jordan didn't make his high school varsity basketball team his first try. Michael Jordan is now believed to arguably be the best basketball player that ever lived.

Colonel Sanders was turned down 1,009 times for his secret KFC recipe. KFC has been in business, serving this recipe, for over 60 years.

Howard Schultz was turned down by 217 investors. Starbucks is now worth over $85 billion… yes another "b."

Steve Jobs was fired from Apple in 1985, the company he built. Apple rehired him in 1997 and he shaped the way we use and even think about technology, even to this day.

Jesus had one of his twelve closest friends betray him. It was part of the process for the redemption of mankind.

Psalm 23:4 NKJV
Yea, though I walk through the valley of the shadow of death, I will fear no evil; For You are with me;

I've had many conversations with pastors and church leaders from around the world and often times I can tell who's gone through something, who is going through something, or who hasn't gone through something just by the vernacular and conversation flow. When you go through something extremely negative, I mean something that could break people emotionally, mentally, financially, relationally, or in any other area of life, it should humble you, if you go through it correctly. Of course, that's extremely simplified. There will be a ton of negative and positive things that will come of it but developing a humble heart, a love for others, and a sensitive heart are things that have developed in me through it all. Hopefully you never have to go through something so devastating but if it does happen, do it knowing that God is with you and He will never fail you. I can testify to this from my own life experience!

Another thought on this verse is that it refers to going through. It does not say anything about staying in the valley of the shadow of death! Some people get so used to their circumstance that they build a mailbox and set up housekeeping there.

YOU ARE NOT CALLED TO LIVE IN THE VALLEY OF THE SHADOW OF DEATH.

You are called to live mountaintop to mountaintop, glory to glory. This life isn't supposed to be easy, at least in my experience, but it is supposed to be enjoyed and felt along the way. I've experienced a lifetime's worth of pain and bad circumstances, but I also know that I went through those things. Going through them instead of them allowing to reside in me has been quite a learning process. When we learn from our bad experience it can do nothing but help us. Experience isn't the best teacher, evaluated experience is the best teacher. There's a huge difference between going through something and something bad happening to us. When we go through, instead of allowing it to happen to us, we become in control of ourselves. Valleys will come and go, but developing our character through those valleys will stay with us. Whatever you are facing, keep pushing through! Feel it all, but get THROUGH it all as well!

I hope by now you've gathered the point of this book. The stuff dreams are made of are not unicorns, rainbows, and warm fuzzies. Dreams are filled with pain, heartache, betrayal, and immense brokenness. When you look at someone who is seemingly living their dream, I can guarantee there are stories of great pain behind them.

So why pay that price? Why put ourselves in the position of getting hurt? Because it's worth it. Living your dream is worth the fight. It's worth the disappointments and setbacks. It's worth the failure and sting of broken relationships. Your dream, God's dream... it's worth it. It may seem dark now, it may seem like your dream is dead and gone but you have to understand, God raises dead things back to life. Don't keep mourning over something you can't change. Don't allow success to go to your head and don't let failure get to your heart. Dreams have a way of helping us get to a new beginning. Sometimes the dream in our mind's eye is the only thing we have going for us! Dreams can gives us hope because they are a pictured of the preferred future that we truly want.

When I went through that darkest season of my life years and years ago, I had lost everything...family, ministry, influence, relationships. My life was in complete devastation. It was like coming out of a shelter after a tornado and looking over the damage. It was horrific. I wasn't sure I was going to make it. I remember the thought process was very bleak. I honestly wasn't sure I wanted to be alive. I wrestled with depression, fear, anger, bitterness, and unforgiveness. People who were the closest in my life were now trying to destroy me.

I had two choices...

Give up or go through.

I could give up on life. I could have said, "Forget church and Christians in general. Forget living for a greater purpose. I'm going to live for me." I could have gone down many self-destructive roads, but something in me just couldn't do it. Call it genuine determination or call it the arrogance of not giving the haters the satisfaction. Call it what you want, but I truly feel the thing that got me through it is Jesus. I don't mean that in a generalized way. I mean it very specifically. Let me explain.

Those people did not knit me together in my mother's womb. Those people did not hang on a brutal cross for me. Those people did not call me into ministry. Those people do not control any part of my life. I'm not accountable to anybody who hasn't walked with me through the fire. If you haven't carried the weight of relationship with me, then your words carry no weight with me! I know that sounds so bad in this Christian world of "accountability," but we need to understand that accountability is a privilege and honor to be earned in someone's life. It isn't anyone's right to hold someone accountable if they don't have a relationship with that person. It doesn't make you unteachable, it makes you wise to receive the right advice from the right people. The people that had my best interest at heart and had earned the right to be there are who kept me through the dark hours. But more than anything else it truly was Jesus and His love and calling on my life. How he kept me is how He will keep you as well.

Jeremiah 29:11 NIV
For I know the plans I have for you," declares the Lord, "plans to prosper you and not to harm you, plans to give you hope and a future.

This is my life verse. Of course I understand the biblical and historical context of the verse but nonetheless, this is a promise from God to all people, all places, for all time. It has kept me moving forward through all of life's challenges. His dream and vision for my life is what kept me from giving up or throwing in the towel. When I had nothing, the dream was still alive. The revelation of who Jesus is and what He wanted to do in me was how I made it through the devastation. Dreams and vision have the power to bring life. When I felt my life was done, Jesus was just getting started. He finally had a broken and willing man He could work with. Just like the dream will have parameters that will keep you restrained and on track concerning your behavior and decisions, it will also keep you moving forward when nothing else seems to be working.

Dreams take time. Dreams never really come quickly. It's interesting to hear people who have done and are doing great things on the earth for the kingdom. I've heard the same great sentiment from these men and women time and time again: I am an overnight success story 30 years in the making. Meaning that just because I seem successful now, I had about 30 years of hell to back it up!

NO ONE IS AN OVERNIGHT SUCCESS.

It takes years of practice, years of learning, years of correction. It takes years and years to see your dream come to pass. Scholars say it took Joseph over 20-25 years from the time he had the dream until the time he saw it fulfilled.

The formula isn't just time. It's time + process + growth. Time is going to move forward. Are you? Time moves forward no matter what. It just keeps ticking away. Our part in the process is growth. If we have a big dream then we need to be big people. The process of the dream is what helps us move forward in growth and see our dream happen!

DREAMS RESTORE PEOPLE

One thing I know is that dreams restore people. Dreams help people pull themselves up by the bootstraps and get on with it. Dreams help us get up every morning and they keep us awake at night about what could be and should be in the world around us. Joseph's dream was coming to pass.

Genesis 41:41-43 NIV
So Pharaoh said to Joseph, "I hereby put you in charge of the whole land of Egypt." Then Pharaoh took his signet ring from his finger and put it on Joseph's finger. He dressed him in robes of fine linen and put a gold chain around his neck. He had him ride in a chariot as his second-in-command, and people shouted before him, "Make way!" Thus he put him in charge of the whole land of Egypt.

Wow! Joseph went from the pit to the prison and now he's in the palace! What a story right? I mean here it is! Joseph's dream came to pass! Right? Or was there more? At this point Joseph is living the life, but his dream wasn't just about him being rich, powerful, and successful. This scripture is not the end! This is just some of the perks of the dream. The dream is about restoration of family and relationships.

The dream is that hearts be reunited and turned back towards each other in a loving and honoring way. For the next few chapters Joseph is working his way back towards restoration, and eventually his whole family is reunited. Joseph was filled with grace, a man of character and integrity. He didn't respond in revenge, he was heartbroken and weeping to see his family reunited. The realization of a dream is to always bring restoration into the lives of others. Our dream should always be others-motivated. Here's the part of the story that brings all of Joseph's pain and turns it into purpose.

Genesis 45:1-8 NKJV
Then Joseph could not restrain himself before all those who stood by him, and he cried out, "Make everyone go out from me!" So no one stood with him while Joseph made himself known to his brothers. And he wept aloud, and the Egyptians and the house of Pharaoh heard it.

Then Joseph said to his brothers, "I am Joseph; does my father still live?" But his brothers could not answer him, for they were dismayed in his presence. And Joseph said to his brothers, "Please come near to me." So they came near. Then he said: "I am Joseph your brother, whom you sold into Egypt. But now, do not therefore be grieved or angry with yourselves because you sold me here; for God sent me before you to preserve life. For these two years the famine has been in the land, and there are still five years in which there will be neither plowing nor harvesting.

And God sent me before you to preserve a posterity for you in the earth, and to save your lives by a great deliverance. So now it was not you who sent me here, but God; and He has made me a father to Pharaoh, and lord of all his house, and a ruler throughout all the land of Egypt.

The major but most often overlooked part of God's dream for Joseph was a restoration of his family! I hope you'll read Genesis 41-45 and see how Joseph was careful and wise to allow the people that hurt him most back into his life. We have to let people back in to our lives at some point if they are repentant, meaning if they have changed. Keeping people out may seem like a safeguard but it could also be pride – the original sin. This is the birthplace of every sin. When we make ourselves god we replace the God who made us. Pride has been the downfall of many leaders throughout the years and has brought much pain to so many people. When we humble ourselves and accept that the world doesn't revolve around us, God shows up with his grace and favor on our lives. Sometimes we just have to let go of the fight and let God take control.

James 4:6 NKJV
But He gives more grace. Therefore He says: "God resists the proud, but gives grace to the humble."

When we humble ourselves to God's great plan and process, His grace overwhelms us. His grace covers us, empowers us, and makes a way for us. The dream God has put on your life is because of His grace. We aren't good enough, pretty enough or talented enough. It's all God all the time!

James 1:17 NIV
Every good and perfect gift is from above, coming down from the Father of the heavenly lights, who does not change like shifting shadows.

It's through God's goodness that we even have a dream. His grace is what propels our dream and His anointing is what grows our dream. The entire restoration of your life and dream is wrapped up in grace. Now ask the question…Am I showing the same grace to people that God has shown me? This is important to ask because God has endless possibilities of how our dream or relationships are going to work out. We have to allow the grace of God to direct our thoughts and behavior because people need it! You need grace and so do I. Living our dream is not for us to prove people wrong. When we live our dream, live it with grace. Don't rub your success in the face of people who could care less anyways. This is how Joseph responded. He operated with wisdom and humility.

One day we should wake up and look around and come to the realization that we are living the dream God has intended for our life. It may not look the way we thought, but it rarely ever does when we are living God's plan for our life. The goal in life isn't to arrive at the dream as if it's a destination, the goal is to live the dream. Your life is the dream. If we are always looking towards the next thing or looking towards the next season of life, we will miss the life God has given us all around. If we have our faces buried in our phones and we don't look up every once in a while we could miss the real life that's going on around us.

THE PROVISIONAL & PERFECT PLANS

God always has a plan for our lives. Maybe you feel liked you've screwed up too many times. You've made too many mistakes. Maybe you feel like God has passed you over. I want you to know that God has more than one plan for your life. He has many plans.

Maybe you have experienced divorce. Divorce does not disqualify God's dream.

Maybe your career is over. Your career isn't the equal to God's dream.

Maybe you've experienced the death of a loved one. God's dream is still alive for you.

Maybe you have lost your children. God's dream for you is restoration.

Life is tough. It just is. We will experience things in our life that will alter how we think, live, and believe. Ultimately though, God has a dream and plan for our lives.

Romans 12:2 NKJV
And do not be conformed to this world, but be transformed by the renewing of your mind, that you may prove what is that good and acceptable and perfect will of God.

I love this verse. It implies levels of knowing God's will for our life – the good, the acceptable and the perfect. Or does it? I used to think if I lived perfect, I'd experience the perfect will of God. Then I screwed up, so perfection was no longer an option, but maybe I'll experience the acceptable will of God.

Then I screwed up more so maybe I'd at least experience the good will of God. Well, then I screwed up some more. So now what? No more will of God? Hopefully you see where I'm going. God's will is not dependent upon our behavior. If you reread the scripture it says that we are to renew our minds first then we will prove the good AND acceptable AND perfect will of God. So there aren't types of God's will or levels of blessing. That's silly. That's not how God works. God's will is always going to be good, acceptable, and perfect.

Regardless of where you are in life, God's plan for you has not changed one bit. You are still loved by God. You are still born with a purpose and destiny. You are still called and gifted to do what God has asked. You are still filled with the Holy Spirit and the resurrection power of God resides in you! It does not matter what you've done, God has His plan still in place for you. You are not so powerful that you can abort God's purpose and dream for your life.

God has a perfect plan for our life, but what happens if we mess it up with our bad choices? What happens if our life just goes off the rails?

From what I've found, it's postponement. God will never abort the plans He has for us, but does that mean we can? I don't think so. I believe God always has His plan waiting for us. It may not be the perfect plan that we had in mind, but in our seasons of brokenness He has a provisional plan meaning that He will provide everything we need for us to reach our destiny.

So if you feel like you've gone way too far or have messed up way too much, take it from me. You haven't. God still has a plan for your life.

> **IN EVERY SEASON AND EVERY SITUATION, GOD HAS A PLAN.**

My prayer for you reading this book is that you will live your God-given dream. My prayer is that God gives you the grace to walk through every valley and experience every mountaintop, all the while marching unfazed towards your dream.

> **THIS IS THE STUFF DREAMS ARE MADE OF.**

PERSONAL NOTES

PERSONAL NOTES

MORE FROM ASHLEY

Getting Up is Ashley's first book. It's an authentic testimony of Ashley's personal struggle with addiction and the victory he found by getting up from his circumstances and moving forward. Using the biblical narrative of King David you will learn how to get up and stay up!

"For though the righteous fall seven times, they get back up"
-Proverbs 24:16

The fact is most people live and die without ever scratching the surface of what they were put on this earth to do because of a moral failure, an addiction holding them back, or living a compromised life with little character or integrity. This book will equip people with a real plan to help them get up from devastating circumstances and fulfill their God-given destiny.

Influential leaders across the nation have called it one of the most practical books on restoration that they've ever read. It's time for you or someone you know to Get Up and live the life God has intended for them.

**FOR BOOKING INFORMATION OR
FOR MORE RESOURCES, PLEASE VISIT
ASHLEYJENSEN.ORG**

www.ingramcontent.com/pod-product-compliance
Lightning Source LLC
LaVergne TN
LVHW051521070426
835507LV00023B/3232